A BRIEFE INTRODUCTION TO THE SKILL OF SONG
BY WILLIAM BATHE

Music Theory in Britain, 1500–1700: Critical Editions

SERIES EDITOR

Jessie Ann Owens, Brandeis University, USA

This series represents the first systematic, carefully reasoned attempt to present the entire range of theoretical writing about music by English, Welsh, Scottish and Irish writers from 1500–1700 in a set of modern critical editions. These editions, which will use original spellings and follow currently accepted practices for the publication of early modern texts, will prove invaluable to scholars who have had previously to rely on facsimiles or the limited availability of original copies.

Also published in this series:

A New Way of Making Fowre Parts in Counterpoint by Thomas Campion
and *Rules how to Compose by Giovanni Coprario*
Edited by Christopher R. Wilson

A Briefe Introduction to the Skill of Song

by William Bathe

Edited and with an Introduction by
KEVIN C. KARNES

ASHGATE

© Kevin C. Karnes 2005

All rights reserved. No part of this publication may be reproduced, stored in a retrieval system, or transmitted in any form or by any means, electronic, mechanical, photocopying, recording or otherwise, without the prior permission of the publisher.

Kevin C. Karnes has asserted his right under the Copyright, Designs and Patents Act, 1988, to be identified as the Editor of this Work.

Published by
Ashgate Publishing Limited
Gower House
Croft Road
Aldershot
Hants GU11 3HR
England

Ashgate Publishing Company
Suite 420
101 Cherry Street
Burlington, VT 05401-4405
USA

Ashgate website: http://www.ashgate.com

British Library Cataloguing in Publication Data
A briefe introduction to the skill of song. –
  (Music theory in Britain, 1500–1700. Critical editions)
  1.Bathe, William. Briefe introduction to the skill of song
  2.Bathe, William. Briefe introduction to the true arte of musicke
  I.Karnes, Kevin
  781

Library of Congress Cataloging-in-Publication Data
Bathe, William 1564–1614.
  [Briefe introduction to the skill of song]
  A briefe introduction to the skill of song by William Bathe / edited by Kevin Karnes.
      p. cm. – (Music theory in Britain, 1500–1700)
  Includes bibliographical references and index.
  ISBN 0-7546-3544-9 (alk. paper)
      1. Music theory–Early works to 1800. 2. Solmization–Early works to 1800. 3. Sight-singing–Early works to 1800. 4. Bathe, William, 1564–1614. I. Karnes, Kevin, 1972– II. Bathe, William, 1564–1614. Briefe introduction to the true arte of musicke. III. Title. IV. Series.

MT5.5..B38 2004
781–dc22

2003062884

ISBN 0 7546 3544 9

Typeset by Manton Typesetters, Louth, Lincolnshire, UK.
Printed and bound in Great Britain by MPG Books Ltd, Bodmin, Cornwall.

Contents

List of Figures	*vi*
Series Editor's Preface	*vii*
Acknowledgements	*viii*
List of Abbreviations	*ix*

Part I. Bathe's *A Briefe Introduction to the Skill of Song*: History, Context, Significance

Towards a History of Bathe's Treatise	3
The Contents: A Reassessment	15
Conclusion: Bathe's Uncertain Legacy	42
Notes	44

Part II. William Bathe, *A Briefe Introduction to the Skill of Song*

Editorial Note	56
Edition	57
Notes	93

Part III. Bathe's *A Briefe Introductione to the True Art of Musicke*: The Extant Text

Andrew Melville's Commonplace Book (University of Aberdeen Library MS 28) and Its Copy of Bathe's 1584 Treatise	101
Relationship between the Treatises	105
Editorial Note	111
Transcription	112
Notes	127
Bibliography	*129*
Index	*135*

List of Figures

1 William Bathe, *A Briefe Introduction to the Skill of Song*, sig. Ai^r. By permission of the William Andrews Clark Memorial Library, University of California, Los Angeles — 2

2 'A generall Table comprehending two parts in one, of all kindes vpon all plaine Songs' from Bathe, *A Briefe Introduction to the Skill of Song*, sig. Bviii^v. By permission of the William Andrews Clark Memorial Library, University of California, Los Angeles — 36

3 The beginning of *A Briefe Introductione to the True Art of Musicke* in Andrew Melville's Commonplace Book, University of Aberdeen Library MS 28, fol. 41^r. By permission of the University of Aberdeen — 103

4 Andrew Melville's Commonplace Book, University of Aberdeen Library MS 28, fol. 48^r. By permission of the University of Aberdeen — 104

Series Editor's Preface

The purpose of this series is to provide critical editions of music theory in Britain (primarily England, but Scotland, Ireland and Wales also) from 1500 to 1700. By 'theory' is meant all sorts of writing about music, from textbooks aimed at the beginner to treatises written for a more sophisticated audience. These foundational texts have immense value in revealing attitudes, ways of thinking and even vocabulary crucial for understanding and analysing music. They reveal beliefs about the power of music, its function in society and its role in education, and they furnish valuable information about performance practice and about the context of performance. They are a window into musical culture every bit as important as the music itself.

The editions in this series present the text in its original form. That is, they retain original spelling, capitalization and punctuation, as well as certain salient features of the type, for example, the choice of font. A textual commentary in each volume offers an explication of difficult or unfamiliar terminology as well as suggested corrections of printing errors; the introduction situates the work and its author in a larger historical context.

Jessie Ann Owens
Louis, Frances and Jeffrey Sachar Professor of Music
Brandeis University

Acknowledgements

My work on this edition had its origins in a seminar on the history of British music theory directed by Jessie Ann Owens at Brandeis University during the autumn of 1996. It was in this forum that I had my first encounters with Bathe's ideas, as well as my first taste of the broader field of the history of music theory in which I have worked ever since. I am grateful to Professor Owens for introducing me to both the subject and the field, for graciously sharing with me her extensive knowledge of them, for bearing good-naturedly many false starts and wrong turns on my part, and for encouraging and enabling my work at every stage of its development.

Over the course of this project, I have also benefited from the advice and encouragement of many others. Among them I must especially thank Reginald Bain, Bonnie Blackburn, Ellen Harris, Antony John, Conny Chen Karnes, Allan Keiler, Minji Kim, Lowell Lindgren and Silvio dos Santos for their help. I am grateful to Jeremy L. Smith for reading portions of my study relating to the publication history of Bathe's text and for answering numerous questions I had about Bathe's publisher Thomas East. I am indebted to Lowell Lindgren for his invaluable comments on an early version of the entire manuscript. I wish to thank Charalambos Sophocleous and Matthew Gunderson for preparing the music examples and Raffaella de Rosa for providing most of the Latin translations.

I am grateful to the William Andrews Clark Memorial Library of the University of California, Los Angeles, for kind permission reproduce all of the images from *A Briefe Introduction to the Skill of Song* that appear in this volume. I wish to thank the University of Aberdeen for permission to reproduce both text and images from Andrew Melville's commonplace book, and especially Michelle Gait of the University's Special Libraries and Archives for facilitating my visit during the summer of 2002 and for assisting my work in many ways.

Kevin C. Karnes

List of Abbreviations

Harman Thomas Morley, *A Plain and Easy Introduction to Practical Music*, ed. R. Alec Harman (2nd edn, New York: W.W. Norton, 1963)
Hill Cecil Hill, introduction to Bathe, *A Briefe Introductione to the True Art of Musicke* (Colorado Springs: Colorado College Press, 1979)
MGG *Die Musik in Geschichte und Gegenwart*, 2nd rev. edn, ed. Ludwig Finscher (Kassel: Bärenreiter, 1994–)
NG II *The New Grove Dictionary of Music and Musicians*, 2nd edn, ed. Stanley Sadie, 29 vols (London: Macmillan, 2001)
STC *A Short-Title Catalogue of Books Printed in England, Scotland, and Ireland, and of English Books Printed Abroad, 1475–1640*, comp. A.W. Pollard and G.R. Redgrave, 2nd edn begun by W.A. Jackson and F.S. Ferguson, completed by Katharine F. Parker, 3 vols (London: The Bibliographical Society, 1986–91)
Wing *Short-Title Catalogue of Books Printed in England, Scotland, Ireland, Wales, and British America and of English Books Printed in Other Countries, 1641–1700*, comp. Donald Wing, 2nd edn by John J. Morrison, Carolyn W. Nelson, and Matthew Seccombe, 4 vols (New York: The Modern Language Association of America, 1994–98)

PART I

Bathe's *A Briefe Introduction to the Skill of Song*: History, Context, Significance

A BRIEFE INTROduction to the skill of SONG:

Concerning the practise, set forth by William Bathe

Gentleman.

In which work is set downe X. sundry wayes of 2. parts in one vpon the plaine song. Also a Table newly added of the comparisons of Cleues, how one followeth another for the naming of Notes: with other necessarie examples, to further the learner.

FABIVS.

Musica est honestum et iucundum oblectamentum, liberalibus ingenijs maxime dignum.

LONDON
Printed by Thomas Este.

Figure 1   William Bathe, *A Briefe Introduction to the Skill of Song*, sig. Ai[r]

Towards a History of Bathe's Treatise

Copies of William Bathe's *A Briefe Introduction to the Skill of Song* began to appear on London bookshelves just as a new market for instructional texts on musical subjects was being cultivated by some of the leading publishers in the city.[1] Although the book was issued without a date on its cover page, Jeremy L. Smith, an authority on the work of Bathe's publisher Thomas East, has recently argued that Bathe's treatise was most likely printed in 1596 – thereby strengthening our confidence in a publication date that had been hypothesized previously by a number of other scholars.[2] If accurate, Smith's assertions, based upon an analysis of both bibliographical and watermark evidence, would place the work among a handful of similar texts that appeared within a very short span of time. That same year, the anonymous *The Pathvvay to Musicke* was published by the fiercely competitive William Barley.[3] In 1597, Peter Short, a relative newcomer to the field, printed Thomas Morley's *A Plaine and Easie Introduction to Practicall Musicke*. Before the appearance of these three books in 1596–97, only three other music textbooks are known to have been published in the English language, and of these only one was an original work intended for a general readership: Bathe's own *A Briefe Introductione to the True Art of Musicke*, printed by Abell Jeffes in 1584.[4]

It is understandable that East, who was among the busiest publishers in Elizabethan London, would have been eager to publish Bathe's second treatise in 1596.[5] As Jessie Ann Owens has observed, Bathe's contemporary Thomas Whythorne noted in his diary that Bathe was among 'the most famous musicians in his time'. It also appears that Morley, who was often outspoken in his criticism of the work of his peers, may have thought highly enough of Bathe's writing to quote from it directly when composing his own *Plaine and Easie Introduction*.[6] Indeed the reputation that Bathe already enjoyed among his peers could only have been bolstered by the publication of *A Briefe Introduction to the Skill of Song*, whose contents comprised a significant pedagogical contribution to the musical culture of late sixteenth-century England in two respects. First, Bathe's text outlines a method of solmization – the means by which the novice singer learned to tune the tones and semitones in a melody – that is not only unlike those described by the theorist's contemporaries either in England or on the Continent but that furthermore appears to anticipate the four-syllable, non-hexachordal solmization method that became standard in England over the course of the seventeenth century. Second, his book includes a numerical method for composing canons that provides rare and perhaps even unique evidence for the use of a kind of combinatorial procedure that has recently been proposed to lie behind the composition of canons throughout the sixteenth century, but that appears, apart from Bathe's treatise, not to have been discussed explicitly by theorists until the mid-1600s.

In spite of his innovative contributions to Elizabethan musical culture, Bathe remains an enigmatic figure historically, and the conditions under which *A Briefe Introduction to the Skill of Song* was written and published remain largely unknown. Before describing his theoretical ideas in detail, I will consider what evidence we can gather about his life and activities as they relate to his musical work, and then attempt to establish a chronology for the complex compilation history of his text. Drawing upon textual, biographical and cultural evidence, I will suggest that the bulk of Bathe's treatise was most likely written a decade or more before it was published – between 1584 and 1586. By considering the printing practices of Bathe's publisher and aspects of the legal climate in which he worked, I will furthermore attempt to provide an explanation for the fact that the treatise was not printed until 1596, and a possible answer to the question of why it was issued without a date on its cover page. Although much of the evidence that can be uncovered about the history of Bathe's text is circumstantial, a careful exploration of this history can shed light not only on Bathe's unique contributions as teacher and theorist, but also on aspects of the print and musical cultures in which he worked.

Smith's argument for a 1596 publication date for Bathe's treatise may help lay to rest a problem that has dogged scholars of Bathe's work for decades. However, it raises in turn a number of other questions about compilation history and authorship that must now be considered. These questions arise because we know that Bathe had permanently emigrated from the British Isles some years prior to this date – either in late 1591 or at the beginning of 1592.[7] In fact, in August 1596, one month before East registered Bathe's treatise with the Company of Stationers in London (an action that was typically undertaken prior to publication)[8] Bathe had already begun his Jesuit novitiate in Belgium. Paul Sherlock, one of Bathe's Jesuit colleagues during this intensive two-year period of initiation into the order, described Bathe as 'dedicated ... to study and the practice of virtue' throughout this period. Sherlock recalled that Bathe 'led a life of strict retirement, great penance, and continual intercourse with God'.[9] Given the nature of his activities and his apparently profound dedication to them during the summer and autumn of 1596, it seems unlikely that Bathe would have been overly concerned with his former life in England at the time, and much less with the singing method that he probably wrote several years earlier. The seeming discrepancy between Bathe's biography and the publication history of his text compels us to examine carefully the available accounts of his early life in England and Ireland, the legal circumstances under which his book appeared, and the musical and pedagogical cultures to which he addressed his work, all in an attempt to account for the origins of the book's contents and their eventual publication. We may begin with a consideration of Bathe's text itself.

Compilation history: textual and biographical evidence

Bathe's text consists of three distinct compositional layers: (1) material taken directly from his 1584 treatise *A Briefe Introductione to the True Art of Musicke*; (2) material newly written, which probably dates from between 1584 and 1586; and (3) material that was most likely not added until some time during or after 1592 – that is, after he had already moved to Belgium to undertake theological training. This third layer does not appear to consist of Bathe's own work, but rather may have been contributed by East.

The first layer of material in Bathe's treatise, the only one that can be dated with certainty, is easy to identify. At the beginning of his discussion of 'naming' pitches in *A Briefe Introduction to the Skill of Song* (on sig. Av^r–Avi^v), we find blocks of text that are borrowed directly from his earlier *A Briefe Introductione to the True Art of Musicke* (1584). Although the latter survives only in the form of a seventeenth-century transcription into Scottish spelling, the direct copying of large passages from the work can clearly be seen in the following examples:[10]

A Briefe Introduction to the Skill of Song (1596)	*A Briefe Introductione to the True Art of Musicke* (1584)[11]
The next thing necessary to be knowne for the right naming of notes, is the place where that note standeth which is named *Vt*. And as by counting vpward and downeward from the cliefe it is to bee knowne where euery note standeth, so it is to be knowne by counting vpward and downeward from that which is called *Vt*, what the right name of euery note is … (sig. Av^v)	The third that is necessary to be knowin for the Richt naming of notes, is the place whair yat note standeth whiche is named ut. and as by counting vpward and dounwarde from the cleife it is knowen where every note standeth, so it is knowin by counting wpward and dounward from that which is callit ut, quhat the Richt name of everie note is … (fol. 43^r)
A Briefe Introduction to the Skill of Song (1596)	*A Briefe Introductione to the True Art of Musicke* (1584)
Two things from these rules are excepted, the one is, that every *re*, should be named *la*, when you ascend to it, or descent from it: and that euery *vt*, should bee named *sol*, which two things are vsed *euphoniae gratie*, and yet this name of *vt*, is most proper to the base or lowest part in the first place. (sig. Avi^v)	Two things from thes rules are excepted, the on is that everye re. should be named la, when yow ascend to it, or descend from it, and that everie ut, should be named sol, whiche tuo things ar wsed euphoniae gratia, and yet this name ut is most proper to the Bas. or lowest parte in the first place. (fol. 43^r)

The title page of Bathe's first treatise, the complete text of which is not preserved in the Scottish transcription but is cited in Sir John Hawkins's *General History of the Science and Practice of Music* (1776),[12] reveals that at the time of its publication Bathe was a student at 'Oxenford'. We can thus establish not only an approximate composition date for the first layer of material in *A Briefe Introduction to the Skill of Song* (1584 or earlier), but we also gain some insight into the author's whereabouts and activities during this period. Biographical evidence such as this will become crucial when attempting to date the second and third layers of the treatise. To this end, it will be helpful to review what little we can gather about Bathe's early life before examining the remainder of his text.

As the Jesuit historian Seán P. Ó Mathúna has noted, the precise nature of Bathe's activities are difficult to trace before he began theological training in Louvain at the beginning of 1592.[13] Bathe's course of study at Oxford and the exact dates of his enrolment there are cases in point. In a sworn autobiographical statement made upon his entry into the Society of Jesus in the autumn of 1595, Bathe recalled: 'I studied humane letters in Ireland; the rudiments of philosophy at Oxford, England; then some theology in Louvain' ('Studui in Hibernia literis humanioribus, in Anglia Oxonii perfunctoriae philosophiae; aliquid Lovanii theologiae').[14] Although there is evidence that Bathe attended St John's College while at Oxford, and despite the fact that we know by his own account that he was enrolled in 1584, no record of his graduation exists.[15] Both Ó Mathúna and Timothy Corcoran, an early twentieth-century Jesuit historian, have suggested that Bathe may have left the school without receiving a degree. They suggest that this may have been prompted by his probable refusal, as a Catholic, to take the verbal oath of allegiance to Elizabeth as head of the Church of England that was required of all Oxford graduates during this period.[16] In any case, Ó Mathúna has established that Bathe was already back in his native Ireland by the time of his father's death in July 1586. Suddenly finding himself the head of a wealthy, landed household, his life took a dramatic turn at this point.

By combing the records of both the State of Ireland and the City of Dublin, Ó Mathúna has found that between August 1587 and the end of 1590 no fewer than six major land transactions were brokered or overseen by Bathe on behalf of his family's estate. In August 1589 Bathe enrolled at Gray's Inn in London to acquire the legal training expected of the head of such a family.[17] During these same years, he was twice called to political service. In March 1587, he was dispatched to Westminster as part of a delegation sent by John Perrott, then Lord Deputy of Ireland, to the Queen's court. While serving in this capacity, he is reputed to have captured Elizabeth's attention with his musical skills, and by presenting her with the gift of a harp. This diplomatic mission ended abruptly with Perrott's dismissal from the post in June 1588. Towards the end of 1591, Bathe once again undertook a political journey, this time to the court of Philip II in Spain, very likely on behalf of Perrott's successor William Fitzwilliam.[18] The last extant record of Bathe's presence on the British Isles places him in Ireland at a gathering of his extended family in August 1591. By the beginning of 1592 he had begun his theological studies in Belgium, and, so far as we can tell, never returned to England.

Ó Mathúna's findings, summarized above, provide an intriguing historical backdrop against which to examine Bathe's activities as a musician, and in particular his work on *A Briefe Introduction to the Skill of Song*. I would argue that Bathe had most likely finished his work on the treatise – the second chronological layer of material – before the period of intense financial, legal and political activity began for him in the summer of 1586. This hypothesis relies on evidence relating to the social requirements and expectations faced by a man in the high social position in which he found himself after the death of his father, and on Bathe's own account of his early life that he left us, albeit inadvertently, in his preface to his 1596 book. In the latter we read:

> In a moneth and lesse I instructed a child about the age of eight yeeres, to sing a good number of songs, difficult crabbed Songs, to sing at the first sight, to be so indifferent for all parts, alterations, Cleues, flats, and sharpes, that he could sing a part of that kinde, of which he neuer learned any song, which child for strangenesse was brought before the Lord Deputie of Ireland, to be heard sing ... There was another, that had before often handled Instruments, but neuer practised to sing (for hee could not name one Note) who hearing of these rules, obtayned in short time, such profit by them, that he could sing a difficult song of himselfe, without any Instructor. There was another, who by dodging at it, hearkning to it, & harping vpon it, could neuer be brought to tune sharps aright, who so soone as hee heard these rules set downe for the same, could tune them sufficiently well. I haue taught diuerse others by these rules, in lesse then a moneth; what my selfe by the olde, obtained not in more then two yeeres. (sig. Aiii^{r-v})

Bathe no doubt included this passage in his treatise in order to advertise the effectiveness of his singing method to potential readers, but his account also tells us a great deal about his life around the time when he wrote his book. In essence, what Bathe describes in this passage is his work as a tutor – a teaching musician of a kind that flourished in Elizabethan England by providing rudimentary private instruction in music to children of wealthy, socially aspiring families.[19] Bathe's account may provide an important clue about the date of his writing for the simple reason that his work as a tutor – however informal it might have been – would not have been compatible socially with the life that he led after the time of his father's passing. This in turn implies that he most likely completed his work on *A Briefe Introduction to the Skill of Song* at some point between the publication of his first treatise in 1584 and the summer of 1586.

In order to substantiate this hypothesis, we may consider briefly the evidence provided about the social value of musical training and the status attained by music tutors by some of the many books devoted to the subjects of social strata and mores that were published in England throughout the sixteenth century.[20] These books, many of which sought to outline a course of proper upbringing for children with ties to nobility or from socially aspiring common families, were widely popular among members of the educated classes.[21] The demand for classic texts like Sir Thomas Elyot's *The Boke Named the Gouernour* (1531) and Sir Thomas Hoby's English translation of Baldassare Castiglione's *The Courtyer* (1561) was such that they were reprinted repeatedly for decades after their original publication.[22]

Significantly, the authors of these books were remarkably consistent in their treatment of the subject of musical proficiency among members of the upper classes. Nearly all of them counselled, for instance, that some degree of musical knowledge is a benefit for the socially aspiring individual. As the anonymous author of *The Institucion of a Gentleman* wrote in 1555:

> It behoueth also suche a gentle man to haue in hym courtly beheauoure, to know howe to treate and interteyn men of al degrees, and not to be ignoraunte how he hymselfe oughte to be vsed of others. To such a Gentilman also sum knowledge in Musicke, or to knowe the vse of musicall Instrumentes is much commendable.[23]

Nearly all of these authors, however, also cautioned their readers against becoming *overly* proficient in the musical arts, and against displaying their musical talents in public. Elyot, for instance, suggested that if a male member of the 'gentle' classes were to display publicly his musical skills, he would risk diminishing the respect that he would otherwise command from more common individuals:

> And if the child be of perfect inclination and towardness of virtue, and very aptly disposed to this science [of music], the tutor's office shall be to persuade him to have principally in remembrance his estate, which maketh him exempt from the liberty of using this science in every time and place: that is to say, that it only serveth for recreation after tedious or laborioius affairs, and [the tutor's duty shall also be] to show him that a gentleman, playing or singing in a common audience, appaireth [i.e., impairs] his estimation: the people forgetting reverence when they behold him in the similitude of a common servant or minstrel.[24]

Castiglione was even more explicit on this point, advising: 'Let our Courtier come to shew his musick as a thing to passe the time withall, and as he were enforced to doe it, and not in the presence of noble men, nor of any great multitude.'[25] Henry Peacham's remarks in *The Compleat Gentleman* (1622) reveal that these attitudes were by no means tempered after the turn of the century. He wrote: 'I desire not that any Noble or Gentleman should (saue his priuate recreation at leasurable houres) prooue a Master in the same [musical performance], or neglect his more weightie imployments.'[26]

A man like Bathe, it seems, would have been just the figure towards whom such cautionary statements were aimed. Bathe was not only a gentleman by birth, but, after the death of his father, he became a gentleman, and even a courtier, by profession. He was doubly gentle, or 'gentle gentle' in the terms of the *Institucion of a Gentleman*. The near unanimity of authors like Elyot and Peacham with respect to the subject of musical proficiency among men of Bathe's social standing must cast doubt on the assumption that Bathe would have been engaged as a singing tutor simultaneously with his service in Elizabeth's court, with his assumption of the legal and fiscal responsibilities of his family's estate, or with his diplomatic mission to Spain. After all, as Whythorne recalled in his autobiography, the music tutor in Elizabethan London was often perceived as little better than a household servant; the job could even entail some of the same chores.[27] This evidence, when read alongside the testimony that Bathe provides in his preface to *A Briefe Introduction to the Skill of Song*, implies that the second layer of material in his book was most likely composed before he embarked upon his new life in the summer of 1586. The bulk of his treatise, in other words, was probably written during the period 1584–86, while he was still free, on account of his youth and the secure financial standing of his family, to pursue at will the musical interests that had so captivated him during his student years at Oxford.

So far, I have argued that Bathe must have completed the first layer of material in *A Briefe Introduction to the Skill of Song* during or prior to 1584, and that the second layer was probably written between 1584 and mid-1586. The third layer was most likely added some time after Bathe left England for the Continent at the end of 1591, by which time he certainly would have completed his own work on the book. If we are to accept this hypothesis we must identify another likely contributor to the compilation of Bathe's treatise, and evidence discovered recently by Owens points directly to Bathe's publisher Thomas East.

As Owens has observed, *A Briefe Introduction to the Skill of Song* contains two harmonized psalm settings that appear in the volume without any apparent connection to the rest of the treatise. Curiously, these settings, of 'O God that art my righteousnesse' (sig. Biv^r) and 'O Lord in thee is all my trust' (sig. Cv^v–Cvi^r), are identical to those that are included in East's *The Whole Booke of Psalmes: With Their Wonted Tunes*, first published in 1592.[28] I would argue that the special historical circumstances under which these psalms were commissioned and published almost certainly exclude the possibility that they were added to Bathe's text before the publication of East's psalter. Since Bathe had permanently emigrated to the Continent by the beginning of 1592, their appearance in *A Briefe Introduction to the Skill of Song* lends support to the theory that Bathe himself had little if anything to do with the final compilation of his text. It was, rather, East who appears to have rounded off the contents of Bathe's book with his own contributions – the four-part psalms – and furthermore oversaw the entirety of its publication.

Historically, the 1592 psalter from which the psalm settings in Bathe's treatise are drawn is extraordinary for several reasons. First, as Nicholas Temperley has observed, East's 1592 volume was the first harmonized English psalter to contain music for all the Psalms of David rather than just a selection, as in the earlier collections harmonized by William Hunnis (1583), John Cosyn (1585) and William Daman (1591), or in the harmonized version of the 'Sternhold and Hopkins' metrical psalter that was published by John Day in 1563.[29] Second, East's psalter was politically provocative with respect to the system of royal patents that governed the publication of musical texts during this period. In his classic study of English music printing, Donald W. Krummel has argued that the printing of East's psalter may have been patently illegal, since Richard Day, as the heir of John Day, enjoyed exclusive monopoly rights to the publication of harmonized psalters, and East had no professional affiliation with him.[30] More recently, Smith has suggested that East may have felt immune to legal challenges on this front since he worked under the protection of the potentially overlapping 'music patent' owned by William Byrd.[31] Whatever the case may have been, however, it is clear that the appearance of East's collection in 1592 would have been seen at the time as posing an overt challenge to Day's ostensible monopoly on the publication of musical psalters.

Finally, East's *Whole Booke of Psalmes* was not only a commercially successful publication (it was reprinted three times)[32] but represented a significant entrepreneurial achievement on the part of the publisher. On the cover of his collection, East described the volume as 'Compiled by sondry avthors', and in his preface he boasted: 'Although I might haue vsed the skill of some one learned Musition, in the setting of these Psalmes in 4. parts, yet for varieties sake, I haue intreated the help of many.'[33] Using the skill of 'some one learned Musition' was exactly what his competitors Henry Denham and John Wolfe had earlier done when they published their own harmonized psalters by Hunnis and Cosyn respectively. Unlike these other publishers, East invited contributions from ten of the most highly regarded musicians of his time, including John Dowland, George Kirbye and Richard Allison. East was rightly proud of this achievement and of his collection – so proud, it appears, that he determined to reprint Kirbye's psalm of lamentation 'O Lord in thee is all my trust' and Edward Blancks's setting of Psalm 4, 'O God that art my righteousnesse', towards the end of Bathe's treatise on singing.

Although both of the settings from East's psalter were apparently reset before being included in Bathe's book, their appearance in the latter has profound implications for the present investigation by virtue of the chronology that it suggests. Significantly, East commissioned the settings by Kirbye and Blancks especially for his psalter, which did not appear until 1592. Since Bathe had already moved to the Continent and begun his theological training in Belgium by the beginning of that year,[34] the psalms were probably not added until some time after Bathe had permanently left the British Isles. It is possible that Bathe never saw East's psalms, and that he might not have been aware that they were published together with his text.

These two psalms, furthermore, may not be the only material added to Bathe's treatise by East. As Owens has observed, a number of other items found towards the end of *A Briefe Introduction to the Skill of Song* also seem incongruous with the rest of the treatise. After the conclusion of the second part of Bathe's singing method, 'The post rules of Song' (sig. Biv^v–Bviii^r), his text continues with 'A generall Table comprehending two parts in one' and an explication of a numerical method for composing works in strict canonic imitation above a plainsong tenor (sigs. Bviii^v–Ciii^v). Six pages later, Bathe provides his readers with ten examples of the kind of canonic composition produced by his method (sig. Cvi^v–Cviii^v). In between the table and the examples, however, we find five pages of unrelated material that not only interrupts Bathe's discussion of canon but that is difficult to justify with the content of the treatise as a whole.[35] The latter includes a list of consonant and dissonant intervals, a poem and the Kirbye psalm, which is not canonic. Table 1 summarizes the complete contents of gatherings B and C of Bathe's treatise; the material in question is italicized.

Table 1 Contents of *A Briefe Introduction to the Skill of Song*, gatherings B and C

Signature	Contents
Bi^r–Biv^r	The Rules of Song. [conclusion]
Biv^r	*[Edward Blancks], 'O God that art my righteousnesse'* [a] *[from The Whole Book of Psalmes: With Their Wonted Tunes (1592)]*
Biv^v–Bviii^r	The post rules of Song.
Bviii^v–Ciii^v	A generall Table comprehending two parts in one [table and explication]
Civ^r–Civ^v	*The names of the Cords for Counterpoint, Descant, and any set Song in how many parts soeuer.*
Cv^r	*De Inuentione. [poem]*
Cv^v–Cvi^r	*G[eorge] K[irbye], 'O Lord in thee is all my trust' [from The Whole Booke of Psalmes: With Their Wonted Tunes (1592)]*
Cvi^v–Cviii^v	10. sundry waies of 2. parts in one vpon the plain song. [examples of compositions described by the 'generall Table']

[a] Italics designate material possibly added by the publisher.

What is immediately striking about the suspect material is the precise location at which it appears in Bathe's book. The list of 'Cords for Counterpoint', which includes such rudimentary information as 'A concord is diuided into an Vnizon. Third. Fift.', appears *after*, rather than before, Bathe's discussion of canonic composition. Significantly, Bathe's excursus on canonic writing is complex and highly technical, and would be entirely incomprehensible to a reader who did not already know how to identify consonant and dissonant intervals.[36] In all of the other English music treatises published during this period, lists of consonances and dissonances appear where we would expect them, at the very beginning of discussions of multi-voice writing; this order is maintained in *The Pathvvay to Musicke*, Morley's *Plaine and Easie Introduction* and Bathe's own *A Briefe Introductione to the True Art of Musicke*.[37] It seems unlikely that any practising musician would have chosen to reserve his treatment of this material until the end of his treatise, or would have approved of its unusual placement within *A Briefe Introduction to the Skill of Song*. The poem immediately following this table is set so as to fill the entirety of sig. Cv^r. The lamentation that follows appears with no explanation as to either its placement or its appearance within the treatise. Finally, on sig. Cvi^v, after an interruption of five pages, the consideration of canon resumes as if no break in the discourse had occurred.

When considered together, the miscellaneous nature of the material found towards the end of Bathe's treatise, its strange placement within his text, the historical circumstances under which some of this material originated, the special meaning that it held for Bathe's publisher, and finally the record of Bathe's own activities during this period all seem to point towards East as the compiler, or at least the supplier, of the third layer of material in *A Briefe Introduction to the Skill of Song*. This layer most likely stems from some time between 1592, when East completed work on *The Whole Booke of Psalmes*, and 1596, when he finally published Bathe's treatise.

Although much of the evidence in support of the proposed three-stage compilation history of Bathe's text is circumstantial, the hypothesis itself is sensible given the publishing circumstances faced by East during the period in question. When Bathe left England for the Continent, he apparently left East with a text that was too large to fit within two octavo gatherings yet too small to fill three. As Smith has noted, the publisher of books in Elizabethan England assumed a great deal of financial liability for the success of his publications, primarily on account of the extraordinarily high cost of paper.[38] We may assume, therefore, that East would have been reluctant to publish *A Briefe Introduction to the Skill of Song* with blank spaces left either at the conclusion of 'The Rules of Song' (the very location where Blanks's psalm was inserted) or in the third and last gathering of the volume (where Kirbye's psalm appears). It so happens, furthermore, that Byrd's music patent, under which East may have found legal protection for the publication of his psalter, expired at the beginning of 1596.[39] Suddenly finding himself unable to print his *Whole Booke of Psalmes* without fear of legal reprisal from Day, East may have been only too eager to take advantage of Bathe's textual shortfall to reprint excerpts from the collection of which he was so proud within a context that was likely to escape the notice of Day.[40] In any case, the history of the psalm tunes in question and the events occurring in Bathe's life during this period make it seem improbable that Bathe himself could have had much if anything to do with the actual publication of his book. If the first layer of his work was written during or prior to 1584 and the second most likely between 1584 and 1586, the final layer was probably not added until sometime during or after 1592, when the author was busy embarking upon a new life far from his ancestral home.

Copyright and publication: the legal context

The compilation history proposed above leaves two important questions unresolved. First, why did East wait until 1596 to publish Bathe's text? And why did he issue the book without the imprint of a date on its title page? A possible answer to the first of these questions, and a hint relative to the second, may found on the pages of the Stationers' Company registers. Here we learn that in the autumn of 1597 – perhaps over a year after he had registered and presumably published *A Briefe Introduction to the Skill of Song* – East succeeded in procuring the legal rights to Bathe's first treatise, *A Briefe Introductione to the True Arte of Musicke*, from its original publisher, Abell Jeffes. An entry dated 31 October 1597 reads:

> Thomas Easte. Entered for his copie vnder th andes of the Wardens, *A Briefe Introductione to the True Art of Musicke*, sett forth by WILLIAM BATHE Student at Oxford. yt was a former copie printed by Abell Jeffes *anno* 1584 And is by him sett ouer to master East as appeareth by his letter written to the wardens to haue it now entred for Master Eastes copye.[41]

It seems curious that East's legal manoeuvrings recorded in this entry would revolve around a title that he probably had no intention of reprinting, given the fact that he had already reprinted portions of *A Briefe Introductione to the True Art of Musicke* within the text of *A Briefe Introduction to the Skill of Song*. It is quite possible, however, that East's motivation for making this entry was legal. His belated registration of the 1584 treatise may have been undertaken in an attempt to protect himself and his work from legal reprisal from Jeffes in a culture known for particularly litigious disputes over intellectual property. Moreover, it may have been East's concerns on this front that caused him to delay publication of *A Briefe Introduction to the Skill of Song* until 1596, and then to issue the book without a date on its title page.

Although the topic of intellectual property rights in Elizabethan England is notoriously complex, studies published by Smith and Krummel shed light on aspects that may be directly related to the present case. The key issue here may revolve around Bathe's direct copying of large portions of *A Briefe Introductione to the True Art of Musicke* into *A Briefe Introduction to the Skill of Song*. Although reusing some of his own earlier material may have seemed natural to Bathe, his decision to do so would have placed East in an awkward position as his publisher. This is because Bathe would no longer have owned the legal rights to this material once it had appeared in print in 1584. Those rights would have instead belonged to his publisher, Abell Jeffes.[42]

It is possible that East became aware of this difficulty at the very start of his association with Bathe and his treatise. In any event, East's 1597 entry in the Stationers' records clearly indicates that he felt a need to acquire the rights to Bathe's earlier work even after he had printed the later text. East's eventual acquisition of the rights to the 1584 treatise may have been part of a scheme designed to protect him from the legal ramifications of infringing, inadvertently or otherwise, upon the property rights of another publisher. Smith has shown that East was often willing to go to great lengths to avoid litigation arising from potential disputes over such questions of intellectual property,[43] and, as he and Miriam Miller have observed, East was 'continually bedeviled with lawsuits' arising from precisely these sorts of issues throughout his career.[44] It may have been that the threat of litigation, whether explicit or not, is what motivated East's belated registration of Bathe's 1584 text. This threat may furthermore help to explain his decision to delay publication of *A Briefe Introduction to the Skill of Song* until 1596 and to issue the book without a date on its title page.

Although we cannot know when East first approached Jeffes about the rights to the 1584 book, it appears that those rights were not as immediately forthcoming as East would have liked. By the mid-1590s Jeffes was nearing the end of a fairly short and undistinguished career as a printer, whose total output consisted of only a small handful of texts with musical notation. Krummel has suggested that Jeffes did not even own his own music type, but instead had to borrow it from John Wolfe.[45] In December 1595 Jeffes ran into trouble with the Stationers' Company for printing a number of 'lewde ballades and thinges verye offensive', and one of his presses was punitively destroyed.[46] Perhaps these difficulties had something to do with Jeffes's eventual willingness to part with the rights to Bathe's first treatise. Whatever the case may be, it appears that these rights were not granted to East until some time after *A Briefe Introduction to the Skill of Song* was published in 1596.

As Smith notes, East was a meticulous printer, and it is exceedingly unlikely that he would have inadvertently published Bathe's book without a date on its cover.[47] I would suggest that by deliberately hiding the actual date of publication during this period of uncertain legal entitlement, East would have been able to print copies of the treatise before his business with Jeffes was settled, without leaving the clear mark of evidence that could be used against him should any litigation arise relative to the case.[48] The entry that East had already made of *A Briefe Introduction to the Skill of Song* on the Stationers' books in September 1596 would not in itself have been enough to incriminate him, since, as Smith has shown, he (and presumably other printers as well) made a habit of registering titles well in advance of actual publication, and especially during periods of lapse in ownership of the royal music patent. Significantly, the first such lapse, which lasted almost three years, began in January 1596.[49]

We may never know why, after already waiting over four years from the time that Bathe had left for the Continent, East apparently decided to go ahead and print *A Briefe Introduction to the Skill of Song* before securing the rights to Bathe's earlier book. Perhaps East was aware that two of his competitors, William Barley and Peter Short, were planning to issue their own music textbooks around this same time, and he may have wanted to beat them to publication.[50] In any case, given the trouble that Bathe's text seems to have caused him, we may assume that East thought highly of its contents, and of the book's potential to earn him a fair amount of money. It is to the nature of these contents that we may now turn.

The Contents: A Reassessment

In *A General History of the Science and Practice of Music* (1776), Sir John Hawkins published a scathing assessment of Bathe's life and work that, as Owens has observed, appears to have set the tone for the reception that *A Briefe Introduction to the Skill of Song* has received among subsequent generations of historians and music theorists.[51] Beginning his discussion of Bathe's work with a cursory consideration of the opening lines of the 1584 treatise *A Briefe Introductione to the True Art of Musicke*, Hawkins wrote:

> The preface was doubtless intended by the author to recommend his book to the reader's perusal, but he has chosen to bespeak his good opinion rather by decrying the ignorance of teachers, and the method of instruction practised by them, than by pointing out any peculiar excellencies in his own work.[52]

Turning to *A Briefe Introduction to the Skill of Song*, Hawkins observed that 'here again the author, according to his wonted custom, censures the musicians of his time, and magnifies the efficacy of his own rules'.[53] Attempting to summarize Bathe's contributions to the practice of solmization, Hawkins continued:

> from the manifold objections of the author to the usual method of teaching, a stranger would expect that [Bathe's own methods] were not only better calculated for the purpose of instruction, but also discoveries of his own; but nothing like this appears: his rule of teaching is the scale with the six syllables, and the cliffs of Guido; the mutations, the stumbling-block of learners, he leaves as he found

them; and, in short, it may be truly said that not one of the 'prolixe circumstances or needlesse difficulties' that others use in teaching, is by him removed, obviated, or lessened.[54]

Although Hawkins's comments on Bathe's work were first published over two hundred years ago, they still seem to resonate with the thinking of many modern scholars who have dismissed Bathe's writings as confused, misleading about contemporary practice and in general too highly touted by Bathe himself.[55]

Bathe's theories, however, are in fact neither confused nor misleading about the practice of solmization in late sixteenth-century England. Indeed, his discussions of these theories can be disorienting for readers not acquainted with the rhetorical strategies of the period (and Hawkins seems to have been one such reader), yet even the most elaborate of the strategies that Bathe employs are not unlike those found throughout the contemporary pedagogical literature on music and other subjects. By examining aspects of the rhetorical traditions within which Bathe worked, we can come closer to understanding the potentially disorienting tactics that he adopts in his book, and, in turn, arrive at a more accurate appreciation of his significant but often misunderstood contributions to the field of music pedagogy. The following discussion of Bathe's rhetorical strategy will serve as a preface to a consideration of the solmization method and the method for composing canons, that together comprise the heart of *A Briefe Introduction to the Skill of Song*.

Bathe's rhetorical strategy

Hawkins's objections to Bathe's work stem primarily from two concerns: his sense that Bathe's theories are self-contradictory in that they purport to offer the student a new and simplified method of learning to sing while at the same time making repeated references to a more traditional hexachordal solmization system; and his annoyance at what could perhaps best be described as the arrogance of Bathe's demeanour. If we examine Hawkins's complaints more closely, however, we find that they address characteristics of Bathe's manner of presentation and argumentation that were not peculiar to Bathe himself but rather were typical for a writer on pedagogical topics in late sixteenth-century England. Rather than reflecting any defensiveness or lack of real understanding of his material, Bathe's approach to writing reveals that he had a thorough understanding of the rhetorical traditions of his time, and of the most effective ways to present his ideas to an Elizabethan audience.

With respect to Hawkins's complaints about the apparent arrogance of Bathe's demeanour, one may assume that the historian had in mind a passage like the following, in which Bathe recounted the rare efficacy of his solmization rules. Boasting of the achievements of his many students, Bathe recalled: 'There was another, that had before often handled Instruments, but neuer practised to sing (for hee could not name one Note) who hearing of these rules, obtayned in short time, such profit by them, that he could sing a difficult song of himselfe, without any Instructor' (sig. Aiii[v]). Elsewhere, comparing his methods to those of earlier teachers, Bathe declared: 'th'effect of my pretended purpose, and fruit of my finished labor is this, where they gaue prolixe rules, I haue giuen briefe rules, where they gaue vncertaine rules, I haue giuen sure rules, and where they haue giuen no rules, I haue giuen rules' (sig. Aii[v]–Aiii[r]). When considering such passages as these, however, it is important to bear in mind that they are far from unique to Bathe's text. Rather, they are found throughout the Elizabethan literature on music, and reflect an author's awareness of the special function that books like *A Briefe Introduction to the Skill of Song* were intended to fulfil within the culture of the period.

Unlike many of the theory texts published by Bathe's Continental contemporaries, many of whom intended their works to be used within a school or another formal instructional context,[56] all the English treatises known to have been published around 1600 were intended by their authors to be used as self-contained tutors, sufficient in themselves to provide for the instruction of musical laymen who might not otherwise have the opportunity to acquire a musical education.[57] Most likely attempting to appeal to the same class of readers who, unable to afford private tutors in their homes, were attracted to the manuals for gentlemanly behaviour that were so popular throughout the period, English writers on music were careful to advertise in their texts the fact that reading their books would provide all the instruction that the aspiring musician would need in order to learn to sing, play an instrument or even compose.

Addressing his work to the 'poore vnlearned and rude', for instance, the anonymous author of the 'Shorte introduction into the science of musicke' that was occasionally included as a preface to John Day's 'Sternhold and Hopkins' metrical psalter wrote:

> I haue set here in the beginning of this boke of psalmes, an easie and most playne way and rule, of the order of the Notes and kayes of singing, whiche commonly is called the scale of Musicke, or the *Gamma vt*. Wherby (any dilige[n]ce geuen therunto) euerye man may in a fewe dayes: yea, in a few houres, easely without all payne, & that also without ayde or helpe of any other teacher, attayne to a sufficient, knowledg, to singe any Psalme contayned in thys Booke, or any such other playne and easy Songes as these are.[58]

Like Bathe, the author of this treatise emphasized at the beginning of his text that the introduction itself suffices to provide all that the beginning student needs in order to learn to sing. He or she argued, also like Bathe, that no actual teacher is required. Along similar lines, Morley claimed the following in 1597:

> As for the methode of the booke, although it be not such as may in euery point satisfie the curiositie of *Dichotomistes*: yet is it such as I thought most conuenient

> for the capacitie of the learner.... . And this much I may boldly affirme, that any of but meane capacitie, so they can but truely sing their tunings, which we commonly call the sixe notes, or *vt, re, mi, fa, sol, la*, may without any other help sauing this booke, perfectly learn to sing, make discant, and set partes well and formally togither.[59]

Here again, the author promises his readers in the introduction to his text that no actual teacher is required for their elementary training in music. Purchasing and reading the book in hand, Morley assured them, would provide all the instruction that they would need.

Continuing along these lines, Morley also proclaimed, again like Bathe, that 'if any at all owe mee any thanks for the great paines which I haue taken, they be in my iudgement, those who taught that which they knew not, and may here if they will learne'.[60] One of the primary reasons that Morley had found for writing his book, he asserted, was to correct the misinformation propagated by other teachers in his day. The lutenist Thomas Robinson began his own textbook, *The Schoole of Musicke* (1603), with a similar statement:

> It is verie true, that manie, both men and women, that in their youth could haue played (for that kinde of play) passing well, in their age, or when they once haue beene married, haue forgotten all, as if they had neuer knowne what a Lute had ment: and the reason I finde to proceed (in the beginning of their learning) from the ignorance of their teachers.[61]

Robinson, like Morley and Bathe, set out when writing his text to offer his students what we can only assume he believed to be a new and better method of instruction than those that were commonly provided in his day. As these and other examples indicate, the lofty claims that Bathe made in the preface to his book – those to which Hawkins objected so strongly – were thus far from unusual, or uncharacteristic, for a writer of the period. Such claims instead seem to have been a fairly typical means of enticing the potential reader (and buyer) to try out the instructional methods presented within the body of a text.

In raising his second objection, that Bathe's explanations appear self-contradictory in that the author purports to offer a new method for solmization while continually making reference to traditional hexachordal practices, Hawkins likewise seems to react more directly to the ways in which the rhetorical traditions of Bathe's time are reflected in his text than to any deficiencies in Bathe's methods themselves. In this case, however, the task of uncovering these traditions and arriving at an understanding of Bathe's rhetorical orientation will require a brief excursion into a subject that his contemporaries called *eloquence*, the art of stating and defending an argument.

In *A Briefe Introduction to the Skill of Song*, Bathe makes extensive use of a rhetorical strategy that writers on eloqence typically called *objection and answer* or *anticipation and confutation*. In essence, this strategy is rooted in the assumption that a text represents a dialogue between writer and reader, and that the writer's task is to anticipate and refute objections that may arise in the reader's mind to arguments laid out by the author.[62] In his 1555 book *A Treatise of the Figures of Grammer and Rhetorike*, Richarde Sherrye summarized its intended effect: 'When perceyuing aforehande an obiection that migt be layde agaynste vs and hurte vs, we wipe it away or euer it bee spoken.'[63] A distinguishing feature of this rhetorical strategy (a feature that seems to have caused Hawkins some confusion) is that it necessitates an author's explicit consideration of views that are incompatible with and even contradictory to his or her own. To be sure, many Continental writers were also fond of framing their theoretical discussions in the form of simple question-and-answer dialogues,[64] but use of the strategy of *objection and answer* as described by Sherrye and employed in Bathe's treatise appears to have been peculiar to the English writers. It was, however, by no means unique to Bathe's work.

In the writings of some, the essential tenets of *objection and answer* are manifested in the form of a fictional discussion between two characters who disagree in their opinions about a subject. The presentation of contravening views that lies at the heart of the strategy is accomplished by assigning these views to various actors in the dialogue. Lodowick Bryskett, writing in 1606 on the value of musical education, presented his case in this manner:

> Let it suffice that yong men are to make great account of that part of Musike which beareth with it graue sentences, fit to compose the mind to good order by vertue of the numbers and sound. ... But this that by varietie of tunes, and warbling diuisions, confounds the words and sentences, and yeeldeth onely a delight to the exterior sense, and no fruit to the mind, I wish them to neglect and not to esteeme.
>
> Indeed (said captain *Carleil*) I agree with you, that our musike is far different from the ancient musike, and that well may it serue to please the eare: but I yeeld that it effeminateth the minde, and rather diuerteth it from the way of blisse and felicitie, then helpeth him thereunto.[65]

Other writers, including the anonymous author of the 1586 book *The Praise of Musicke* (sometimes attributed to John Case),[66] made explicit reference in their texts to the elements of *objection and answer* as described by Sherrye and other rhetoricians. The very title of the twelfth chapter of *The Praise of Musicke* bears this out: 'A Refutation of obiections against the lawful vse of Musicke in *the Church*.' In recounting his motivation for framing the discussion of this subject according to the principle of *objection and answer*, the author wrote:

> In the last part of my treatise I might seem to vndertake a matter far aboue my ability: were it not that either their obiections were too weake to proue theyr purposes: or those which are of any force, mistaken and grounded vpon false principles. Neuerthelesse that I may proceede orderly therein, it shall not be amisse, to see what diuersity of opinions are concerning this matter.[67]

Here again, the consideration of differing and even contravening views lies at the heart of the rhetorical strategy that the author employs.

It may be that no sixteenth- or seventeenth-century writer on music published a book that is more deeply permeated with the strategies and vocabulary of contemporary rhetorical practice than Bathe. His method of argumentation, however, is nonetheless similar to those employed by Bryskett, the author of *The Praise of Musicke*, and others. An example from Bathe's treatise may serve to illustrate this point. On sig. Avi[v]–Aviii[v] of *A Briefe Introduction to the Skill of Song*, Bathe describes a method by which a beginning singer can learn to tune notes altered by accidental sharps. He defends the theoretical basis of his method by means of the objection-and-answer paradigm described by Sherrye and others. He even labels the rhetorical steps by which he proceeds: *Obiection against the latter exception, Solution, Resolution*, and so on. Bathe's argument in this case is that the appearance of accidental sharps should not affect the solmization of a passage.[68] The contravening opinion – the imagined voice behind the objections – holds that all notes preceded by sharps should be called *mi* regardless of their natural place within the scale.

Like the author of *The Praise of Musicke*, Bathe prefaces his argument with an explanation of how he will proceed, and a justification of his use of the rhetorical method of *objection and answer*. After acknowledging the opinion against which he will argue (that all sharp notes should be called *mi*), he writes:

> And because of that opinion there bee so many, I will for them shew a probable reason as by our principles may be shewed: Then after by resoluing them, shewe what is most profitable, not refuting the opinion as an errour, beecause that looking to the matter, wee may finde that they may bee named as well *mi*, as *fa*, insomuch as the names (as I sayd before) are no necessary accidents, but neuerthelesse, because heere we seeke the most apt name, it were vnfit to passe it ouer. Wherefore the principall argument for them wee may in this sort forme. (sig. Avii[r])

In order to defend his own views on the subject, Bathe will attempt to address, at every stage in his argument, the scepticism and contravening views of those potential detractors among his readers. By doing so, he intends, as Thomas Wilson wrote in *The Arte of Rhetorike* (1563), to 'preuent those words, that another would saie, and dispose them as vntrue or at least wise answere vnto them'.[69]

After stating his belief that notes marked by accidental sharps may be named *fa* just as well as *mi*, Bathe presents, as Wilson would advise, three arguments for the contrary opinion, that 'euery note hauing a sharpe beefore it, should be named *mi*'. Rhetorically challenging his own opinion about the subject, Bathe reasons that (1) 'no note that is sharp in the *gamvt* is named *fa*, therefore no note made sharp by collaterall reason [that is, by the addition of an accidental sharp], should bee named *fa*'; (2) 'throughout all the *gam vt*, from *sol* to *fa*[,] Next vnder it is a whole note [in other words, the distance between *sol* and *fa* on the gamut is a whole tone], but from that *sol* to that *fa* [raised by an accidental sharp], if we should call it *fa*, is but a half note, therefore if we call it *fa*, wee breake altogether the rule of *gamut*, which wee should obserue'; and (3) 'euery place in the *gam vt* that is sharp, is named either *mi* or *la*', and therefore should under no circumstances be called *fa* (sig. Avii^{r-v}).

After laying out these potential challenges to his own view, Bathe proceeds to dismantle each in turn. He argues that (1) 'seeing that no sharp note in all the *gam vt* is named *fa*, we may impute an other absurditie to them, seeing they would haue the next note vnder *sol* [to be named not *fa* but] *mi*, which is not found in all *gam vt*, which is the more absurditie'; (2) 'as euery *sol* to *fa*, next vnder it is a whole note: so from euery *sol* to *mi*, next vnder it is more [than a whole tone]: so that according to the *gam vt*, in that respect none of them is true' (in other words, if the sharp note directly under *sol* were called *mi*, the syllables would imply that the interval between the two would not be a semitone, as the accidental sharp would imply, but rather something greater than a whole tone); and (3) insisting upon naming all sharp notes *mi* can give rise to a situation in which alternating pitches (such as B and C♯ when *ut* is G) are both named *mi*, which 'would make them seeme as though it were *mim, mim, mim* ... wherby it plainely appeareth that this is most absurd' (sig. Avii^v–Aviii^r).[70] Having thus discredited all three arguments that one could plausibly make against his own opinion, Bathe has freed himself to restate and construct a theoretical justification for his own view – that sharps do not affect solmization – without, presumably, any further challenges arising in the reader's mind.

Given that the stated programme of Bathe's work was to present a new and more effective method of teaching beginning musicians to sing (and thus to challenge a number of well-established contravening views on the subject), the use of the rhetorical strategy of *objection and answer* that Bathe adopts in his treatise would have seemed natural for an educated Elizabethan gentleman fluent in the rhetorical traditions of his time. This strategy is one that was both well documented in the contemporary literature on rhetoric and moreover appeared in a variety of guises in books on music and other subjects published around the turn of the seventeenth century. Ironically, this same strategy, which necessitates an explicit consideration of contrasting and even contradictory arguments and viewpoints, can lead the modern reader, unfamiliar with these rhetorical traditions, to conclude that Bathe is inconsistent, that his arguments are contradictory, and that he misunderstood the subjects about which he wrote. The actual case, as I will argue as we turn to a consideration of Bathe's theories themselves, is in fact just the opposite.

A simplified solmization method: beginnings of a four-syllable system

In *A Briefe Introduction to the Skill of Song*, Bathe made three important contributions in the area of singing pedagogy. He outlined a solmization method that employs a fixed sequence of syllables spanning an octave and that eliminates the need for a singer to think in terms of hexachords and mutations in order to tune a passage of music correctly; he provided a set of concrete guidelines to help singers negotiate passages marked by accidental flats; and he offered a method by which singers could learn to tune notes altered by accidental sharps. With respect to all three of these issues, Bathe was the first English writer to provide explicit advice to his readers. Furthermore, the four-syllable, non-hexachordal solmization method described in his text is not only fundamentally different from those methods discussed by his English peers and apparently in common use during his time, but also anticipates directly the four-syllable methods that became standard in England after the turn of the seventeenth century.[71]

Before considering Bathe's theories themselves, it is necessary to comment briefly on the overall structure of his treatise. Throughout, the text is divided into two large sections, 'The ante rules of Song' (sigs. Aiv^r–Biv^r) and 'The post rules of Song' (sigs. Biv^v–Cv^r). He explains this division with a reference to Aristotle: 'As Aristotle in setting forth his predicaments, saw many things requisite to be entreated off: and yet vnfit to be mixed with his treatise: he therefore made ante predicaments, and post predicaments: so I for the same cause (desirous to abolish confusion) haue added to my rules, ante rules, and post rules' (sig. Aiii^v). Unfortunately, Bathe's explanation provides little insight into his intentions. Aristotle's *Post-Predicaments*, as the second part of his *Categories* was commonly known during Bathe's time, has generally been considered by modern scholars to be inconsistent with the first part of the treatise. It appears to have been a later addition to Aristotle's text, and its authenticity has even been called into question. Moreover, the term *Post-Predicaments* was not used by Aristotle himself.[72] I believe that Bathe intended this division to represent something similar to what Morley had in mind when he wrote the 'Annotations' to his *Plaine and Easie Introduction to Practicall Musicke*: the 'ante rules' contain basic instructions necessary for singing, and the 'post rules' provide supplementary information and insight into more advanced topics.[73] Since the significance of this division is unclear and, in any case, not crucial to developing an understanding of Bathe's theories and methods, I have chosen not to emphasize this distinction in the discussion that follows.

Bathe's primary contribution to English music pedagogy, his basic solmization method, is founded upon an observation that he first published in his 1584 treatise *A Briefe Introductione to the True Art of Musicke*. Here he noted, like countless writers before him, that the interval series expressed by the ascending sequence of six solmization syllables *ut, re, mi, fa, sol* and *la* – with the characterisitc semitone between *mi* and *fa* – provides an invaluable tool for the beginning singer in that it enables him or her to identify the location of whole and half steps in a melody when it is mapped onto the vocal line of a new or unfamiliar composition.[74] At the beginning of his discussion, Bathe observes that the transpositional level at which the series of syllables should be sung (in other words, the note on which one should sing the syllable *ut*) can be determined by the presence or absence of flats in the passage that one is attempting to tune.[75] Bathe discussed this issue without fanfare in his 1584 treatise, but when he addressed it in *A Briefe Introduction to the Skill of Song* he marked it off from the body of the text with the heading 'The rule of Vt':

The rule of Vt

The next thing necessary to be knowne for the right naming of notes, is the place where that note standeth which is named *Vt*. And as by counting vpward and downeward from the cliefe it is to bee knowne where euery note standeth, so it is to be knowne by counting vpward and downeward from that which is called *Vt*, what the right name of euery note is: but first let vs set downe how the place where the *vt* standeth is knowen, which is this. There be three places, in one of which the *vt* must alwaies be: that is to say, in *G*, which is *Gamut* and *G sol re vt*, when there is no flat[;] in *C*, which is *C fa vt*, *C sol fa vt*, and *C sol fa*, when there is a flat in *b mi* or *b fa b mi*. In *F* which is *F fa vt*, when there are two flats, one in *b mi* or *b fa b mi*, the other in *E la mi*, or *E la*.

As for example.

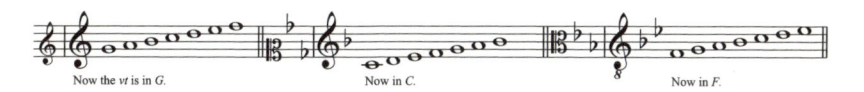

¶ No b flat, the *(vt)* in G. The b flat in b onely, the *(vt)* in C. The b flat in b and E, the *(vt)* in F. (sig. Av^v–Avi^r)

At first glance, Bathe's directions for finding the location of *ut* and the appropriate transpositional level for the series of syllables seem to have affinities with the solmization methods described by many Continental writers. In a typical Continental explication, such as that provided by Lucas Lossius in his *Erotemata musicae practicae* (1563), the six syllables are understood to represent a hexachord, which can be sung in three locations: with *ut* on F, with *ut* on C and with *ut* on G.[76] A flat placed before the pitch B in a melody indicates that the singer should tune that melody by using the F hexachord, which Lossius called *bmol*. If a natural sign appears before the pitch B, the singer will know to use the G hexachord, called ♮*dur*.[77] Although the idea of drawing a connection between the location of the syllable *ut* and the presence or absence of flats in a passage is not unique to Bathe's treatise, several things are indeed remarkable about his presentation.

First, as both Owens and Timothy A. Johnson have observed, it is significant that Bathe, unlike Lossius and most other Continental writers (and also unlike Morley or the anonymous author of *The Pathvvay to Musicke*), does not conceive of the six solmization syllables as comprising a hexachord. Rather he fixes their order in such a way as to span an octave.[78] He calls this arrangement of syllables the 'order of ascention & descention'. He writes (sig. Aiv[v]):

> There bee sixe names, Vt, Re, Mi, Fa, Sol, La. The order of ascention & descention with them is thus.

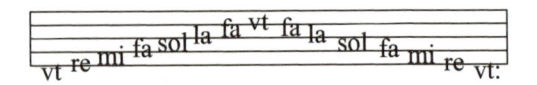

He continues by proposing an 'exception' to this order: he suggests that the names *ut* and *re* should be changed into *sol* and *la* unless they refer to the lowest pitches in a passage (sig. Av[r]):

> *Exceptions.*
>
> Change Vt, into Sol, change Re, into La, when the next remouing Note is vnder.

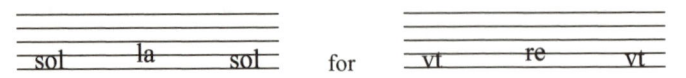

If the student follows Bathe's advice in this regard (and Bathe himself is somewhat inconsistent in this respect), the solmization system that results will consist of a fixed sequence of four syllables arranged so as to span an octave, with the syllable *fa* assigned to the upper note of each adjacent pair of notes separated by a semitone.[79] This is the same four-syllable octave series, shown in Example 1, that we find in Thomas Campion's well-known treatise *A New Way of Making Fowre Parts in Counter-Point* (*c.*1613). Moreover, this is the same system that became the standard in England throughout much of the seventeenth century.[80]

Example 1   Bathe's 'order of ascention' with *ut* on G, C and F

Other aspects of Bathe's discussion are also worth noting. First, as Owens and Johnson have previously observed, Bathe not only carefully avoids presenting the syllables in his text in a hexachordal arrangement, but futhermore defines his 'orders of ascension' according to pitch collections that are essentially different from those that Continental theorists typically called the soft, natural and hard properties.[81] Whereas Sebald Heyden, for instance, noted in *De arte canendi* (1540) that the use of the soft hexachord, with *ut* on F, is indicated by the presence of a single 'b' (signifying a flat) written at the beginning of a line of music,[82] Bathe's 'order of ascention' beginning on F is indicated by the presence of *two* flats – on B and E. Such an account would never occur in a typical Continental discussion, since the pitch E, whether natural or flat, is beyond the range of the soft hexachord and was not associated with it in an integral way.[83] The 'order of ascention' that Bathe constructs, on the other hand, spans an octave, and therefore necessitates the assignment of a syllable to the seventh pitch above *ut*. In the standard 'order of ascention' as Bathe describes it, the interval between the sixth and seventh pitches is a semitone, and so the seventh pitch (E♭ when *ut* is F) is named *fa*. In this way, Bathe's three 'orders of ascention' may be considered representations of three distinct and perhaps uniquely English pitch collections, which Owens has characterized as no-flat, *ut* = G; one-flat, *ut* = C; and two-flat, *ut* = F.[84]

Of equal significance is Bathe's inclusion of the flat sign (♭) in his list of clefs (sig. Av^r–Avi^v), which allows him to elaborate upon 'The rule of Vt' in such a way that he can provide readers with guidelines to find the location of *ut* in any passage simply by considering the clef or combination of clefs that appear at its beginning. His first directive along these lines is that 'G putteth *Vt* to the same place'; by this he means that the presence of a G clef, in the absence of any signature flats, indicates that *ut* is G. He continues with two further directives: 'F. and B. to the next vp'. An F clef with no signature flats indicates that *ut* should be sung one note higher than that on which the clef stands – that is, on G. Similarly, a B clef (a signature flat) alerts the singer to the fact that he should sing *ut* on C, the note the 'next up' from that on which the B clef stands. The fourth rule Bathe provides is 'C putteth *Vt* to the fift place vp, and from C down to the fourth. B, taketh place of the rest.' By this he means that a C clef without a signature flat indicates that *ut* should be sung on G, a fifth above or a fourth below the location of the clef. A signature flat, however, takes precedence over all other clefs for the purpose of finding *ut*, and will alone determine where the student should sing that syllable. In all, Bathe provides his readers with eight such directives by which they may find the location of *ut* when presented with any combination of clef or clefs, which I summarize as follows:

1. A G clef, in the absence of any signature flats, indicates that *ut* is G.
2. An F clef, in the absence of any signature flats, indicates that *ut* is G.
3. A single B clef – a signature flat on B – indicates that *ut* is C.
4. A C clef, in the absence of any signature flats, indicates that *ut* is G. If there is a signature flat present, however, the reader should use it, rather than the G, C or F clef, in order to determine the location of *ut*.

5. If there are two signature flats a fourth apart (on B and E), the upper flat (on E) should be used in order to find the location of *ut*. Recalling that a signature flat indicates that *ut* should be sung on the note 'next up' from where the flat is located, the student would find that *ut* in such a passage is F.
6. If there are two signature flats a fifth apart (on E and B), the lower flat (on E) should be used in order to find the location of *ut* (in other words, *ut* is F).
7. A D clef, in the absence of any signature flats, indicates that *ut* is G (a fifth below D).
8. If there are two signature flats a second apart (on A and B), the lower flat (on A) should be used to find the location of *ut* (in other words, *ut* is B♭).

By describing a solmization system that fixes the order of syllables within the span of an octave, Bathe is able to provide his readers with a method for recognizing the location of whole and half steps in a melody that eliminates the need to mutate between hexachords whenever the melodic line moves beyond the compass of a major sixth. Moreover, he provides his students with a set of guidelines by which they can find the unchanging position of *ut* simply by noting the presence or absence of signature flats before they even begin to sing. A number of examples from Bathe's treatise, shown in Example 2, can serve to demonstrate his method.

Example 2   Bathe, *A Briefe Introduction to the Skill of Song*, sig. Biii[v]

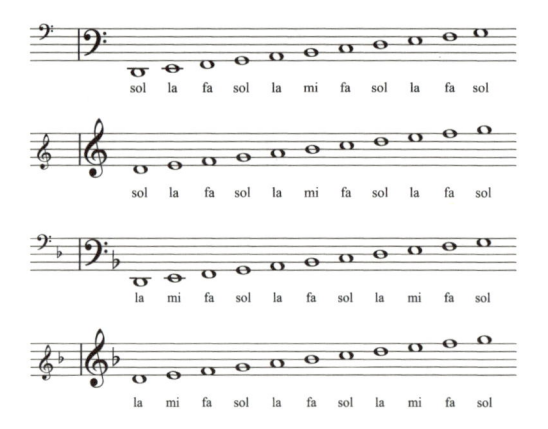

[musical notation: four lines of music with solmization syllables]

Line 1 (bass clef): sol la fa sol la mi fa sol la fa sol
Line 2 (treble clef): sol la fa sol la mi fa sol la fa sol
Line 3 (bass clef with flat): la mi fa sol la fa sol la mi fa sol
Line 4 (treble clef with flat): la mi fa sol la fa sol la mi fa sol

In the first and second lines of music, there are no signature flats. By recalling Bathe's guidelines for finding the location of *ut* from the type of clef found at the beginning of a passage, the singer would recognize that the *ut* in the first line is G (an F clef indicates that *ut* should be sung on the note 'next vp' from the one on which the clef stands). In the second line, *ut* is also sung on G, since a G clef 'putteth *Vt* to the same place'. In both of these examples, *ut* and *re* have been renamed *sol* and *la*, and both are solmized according to the standard four-syllable 'order of ascention' beginning on G: *sol* (G), *la* (A), *mi* (B), *fa* (C), *sol* (D), *la* (E), *fa* (F), *sol* (G). In the third and fourth lines of the example, the B flat 'taketh place of the rest', indicating that *ut* should be sung on the note 'next vp' from that on which the flat stands – on C. Again, *ut* and *re* have been renamed *sol* and *la*, and the passage is solmized according to the standard 'order of ascention' beginning on C: *sol* (C), *la* (D), *mi* (E), *fa* (F), *sol* (G), *la* (A), *fa* (B♭), *sol* (C).

In order to illustrate the profound effect that Bathe's system, with its elimination of the need to think in terms of hexachords and mutations, would have had upon the thinking of a student who had earlier attempted to learn to sing according to more traditional methods, we may consider an example from John Day's famous 'Sternhold and Hopkins' metrical psalter. Beginning in 1569 and continuing sporadically throughout the first part of the seventeenth century, Day printed a number of editions of his best-selling psalter using so-called 'solfège type', a typeface that includes a letter, indicating a solmization syllable, next to each notehead.[85] By publishing his pre-solmized psalters, Day intended, in his words, to help the singer of his psalms to 'knowe how to call euery Note by his right name, so that with a very little diligence ... thou mayst the more easelie by the vewing of these letters come to the knowledge of perfecte *Solfyng:* wherby thou mayst sing the Psalmes the more spedely and easlier'.[86] The editions of Sternhold and Hopkins that were printed using solfège type are particularly valuable for our purposes, since may assume that the syllables that are provided for these tunes reflect common solmization practice in England during the late sixteenth century. If this were not the case, then we could be sure that Day, in keeping with the custom of Elizabethan writers on music, would have been only too eager to advertise the fact that a new and better method of solmization was exemplified on the pages of his book.

Given the history and intended function of Day's pre-solmized psalters, it is revealing that the solfège syllables provided for many of his psalms do not match those that would be prescribed by an octave-based system like the one described in Bathe's *A Briefe Introduction to the Skill of Song*. Rather, the solmization provided by Day appears to derive from a hexachordal system, or from a system like Morley's, which Owens has shown to be closely related to those systems commonly employed on the Continent.[87] In Example 3, a transcription of Psalm 31 ('Lord geue thy iudgementes'; sig. Dvii[r] in the 1569 edition of *The Whole Booke of Psalmes*), Day's solmization is indicated immediately under the staff. Just below that are shown the syllables that would be prescribed by Bathe's method.

In the case of Psalm 31, the discrepancies between the solmization prescribed by the two systems relate to the pitch E, marked in Day's psalter

Example 3 'Lord geue thy iudgementes' from *The Whole Booke of Psalmes* (1569). Solmization as provided by Day and according to Bathe's method

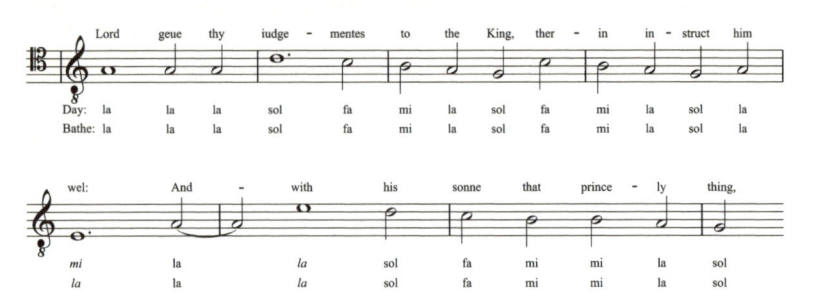

[Musical notation with text underlay:]

Lord — geue — thy — iudge-mentes — to — the — King, — ther-in — in-struct — him
Day: la   la   la   sol   fa   mi   la   sol   fa   mi   la   sol   la
Bathe: la   la   la   sol   fa   mi   la   sol   fa   mi   la   sol   la

wel: — And — with — his — sonne — that — prince-ly — thing,
     mi   la   *la*   sol   fa   mi   mi   la   sol
     la   la   *la*   sol   fa   mi   mi   la   sol

with the syallable *mi* in the lower octave and *la* in the upper; these syllables are italicized in the example. The solmization provided by Day indicates that the singer should begin in the natural hexachord and mutate, between the third and fourth notes, to the hard hexachord, in which he or she should sing the pitches D, C, and B that follow ('iudge-mentes to'). At the return of the pitch A, on the word 'the', the singer mutates back to the natural hexachord, in which he or she sings both the A and the following G ('the Kyng'). The C and B that follow ('ther-in') would require another mutation back to the hard hexachord, after which the singer returns once again to the natural hexachord for the following A and G ('in-struct'). The first appearance of the low E (italicized in the example) is sung *mi*, since it is the third degree of the natural hexachord in which the singer is then operating. However, the high E that appears two notes later ('with') is beyond the compass of the natural hexachord, and requires a mutation back to the hard hexachord in which it is the sixth degree and thus takes the name *la*. The singer trained in accordance with hexachordal methods would continue to tune the remainder of this psalm in a similar manner, mutating between hard and natural hexachords whenever the melody reaches above the compass of the latter or below the compass of the former. In Example 4, I have indicated the mutations that would be required of such a singer when attempting to negotiate this passage.

The relative simplicity of Bathe's system becomes apparent when we trace the steps that a student of his method would take when attempting to solmize this same passage of music. Realizing that the psalm is notated with a C clef and that no flats appear at its beginning, Bathe's student would immediately recognize that *ut* is G. He or she would then proceed to name all of the pitches in the tune according to the standard 'order of ascention' beginning on that note. After renaming *ut* and *re* as *sol* and *la*, the syllable associated with every pitch in the psalm would be fixed – all Gs would be *sol*, all As *la*, and so forth. Because of the duplication of syllables at the octave, the student

Example 4 'Lord geue thy idugementes'. Hexachords indicated below the staff

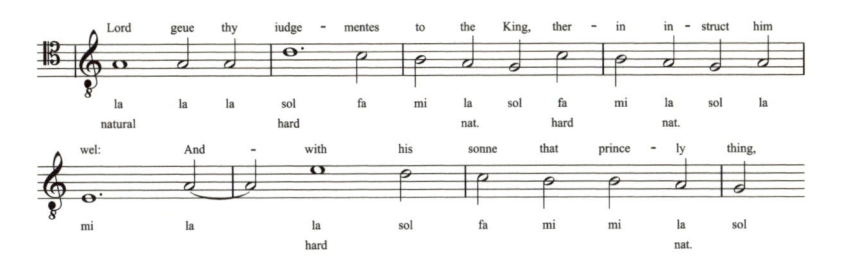

would sing both the upper and the lower E as *la*; only B would be sung *mi*. Whereas the Continental system requires constant attention to melodic ambitus and hexachordal relationships, Bathe's system requires only a single problem to be solved (finding the location of *ut*), and this is handled before the student even begins to sing. As long as no accidental sharps or flats appear in the passage, Bathe's student is freed from having to make any further decisions about solmization and tuning.

A simplified solmization method: tuning accidental flats and sharps

Accidental flats and sharps do, of course, appear frequently in the published music of late sixteenth-century England, and Bathe's *A Briefe Introduction to the Skill of Song* was the first English text to provide its readers with specific guidelines for tuning them. For Bathe, such accidentals presented two distinct theoretical problems that required distinct solutions – one for flats and another for sharps. Both solutions, however, derive from his basic solmization method and 'The rule of Vt'. He began by considering the appearance of accidental flats. He states (sig. Bii[r]):

> If the note to which you goe bee altered by some intermingled flat, then for comptings sake name the Note from which you goe, as well as the note to which you goe, according to the *Vt*, of that intermingled flat, and in so doing take great care not to loose the tune of the note from which you compt, as

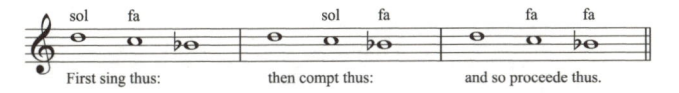

When encountering the first measure of Bathe's example, the singer would recognize, by recalling the 'Rule of Vt', that the syllable *ut* should be sung on G (as indicated by the presence of the G clef and the absence of any signature flats). The B♭ that immediately appears, however, is not found in the 'order of ascention' beginning on G; it does not belong, in other words, to the no-flat, *ut* = G system. Rather, as Bathe explained earlier in his treatise, the appearance of a flat on B (a B clef) indicates that *ut* is C (that the one-flat, *ut* = C system is now in use). The singer, recognizing this fact, must adjust his or her solmization of the passage to reflect this change in the location of *ut*.

Bathe illustrates this process in his example shown above. The singer solmizes the beginning of the passage according to the 'order of ascension' with *ut* on G. Then, in order to tune the altered note correctly ('for comptings sake'), he or she names both the altered note and the one that precedes it according to the new order of ascension, with one flat and *ut* on C; C thus becomes *sol* (since *ut* and *re* are renamed as *sol* and *la*), and B♭ becomes *fa*. This renaming enables the singer to tune correctly the whole tone that lies between C and B♭. Finally, after correctly tuning this whole tone as *sol–fa*, the singer must go back and realign the syllables so that they reflect the 'orders of ascension' to which the notes properly belong: the first two pitches belong to the order with no flats and *ut* on G, and the third pitch belongs to the order with one flat and *ut* on C. The location of *ut* does not actually change, in other words, until the B♭ appears.[88] Presumably (although Bathe is not explicit on this point), the experienced singer would learn to recognize a departure from the original order of ascension somewhat in advance of the event itself, and would be able to solmize a passage such as this without the intermediate second step.[89] Somewhat later in his treatise, Bathe provides his readers with a number of solmized examples demonstrating the negotiation of passages in which the location of *ut* changes repeatedly. One of these passages is shown in Example 5; I have indicated the 'orders of ascension' employed.[90]

Example 5 Bathe, *A Briefe Introduction to the Skill of Song*, sig. Biv[r]. 'Orders of ascension' indicated below the staff

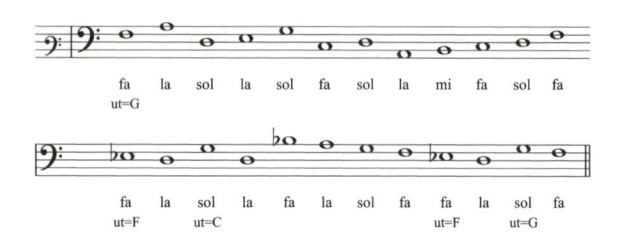

Turning to the subject of accidental sharps, Bathe again explains his method of tuning with reference to the 'Rule of Vt'. He writes:

> If the Note to which you goe, be altered in tune by some intermingled sharp, obserue both in the note from which and to which you goe, this Rule. Compt to the tune of sharps by the Vt, put down to the third place, when you haue thus

compting by wrong names gotten the right tunes, giue the right names after, as (sig. Bii^r):

| la sol | fa mi | sol fa |
| First sing thus: | then compt thus: | and so proceede thus. |

The mental process by which the student of Bathe's method would tune notes altered by accidental sharps is similar to that required to tune notes altered by accidental flats. He or she would begin by singing the passage according to the 'order of ascention' indicated by the clef or combination of clefs at its beginning. When a sharp is encountered, the singer *imagines* (again, 'for comptings sake') that *ut* is located on the third scale degree below the altered pitch. This enables him or her to tune the semitone between the altered pitch and the one above with the syllables *mi–fa*. Finally, after having tuned the semitone correctly by means of these imagined syllables ('by wrong names [having] gotten the right tunes'), the singer must go back and rename all the notes in the passage according to the original 'order of ascention' as found by the 'Rule of Vt'. Although the singer must imagine that the location of *ut* has changed in order to tune the passage correctly, accidental sharps, unlike accidental flats, do not effect any actual change in solmization.

As Owens has observed, the discrepancies that exist between Bathe's treatment of accidental flats and accidental sharps are particularly revealing of the author's conception of the pitch structure of the music that his students would have been learning to sing.[91] For Bathe, the appearance of an accidental flat seems to indicate that the pitch collection employed in a work, as defined by the number of flats and signified by the 'order of ascention' (which is in turn signified by the location of *ut*), has changed. The appearance of an accidental sharp, on the other hand, is an event of merely local or 'surface' significance, and indicates that no such change in the underlying pitch collection has occurred. Although there were many on the Continent who argued similarly that sharps do not affect the solmization of a melodic line, and although Morley, by means of example, seems to concur,[92] Bathe appears to have been among the first writers to propose a theoretical justification, however oblique, for this discrepancy.

In *A Briefe Introduction to the Skill of Song*, Bathe devotes a lengthy discussion, framed according to the rhetorical strategy of *objection and answer*, to precisely this issue. He explains that: 'Of the flat so comming, and of the sharp, there is not like reason, because that the flat so comming should alter the *vt*.' Proceeding according to the objection-and-answer paradigm of argumentation, Bathe continues by considering a potential objection to the foregoing explanation. He concedes that: 'It is graunted that by the last solution [that is, Bathe's explanation], that the flat so comming should alter the *vt*, but to alter the *vt*, doth alter the key (which is in musick a great absurditie).' He concludes his argument by revealing his *solution* to the objection just stated: 'It is graunted conditionally, that is to say, if the like happened (as in the argument obiected) though sometimes in the middest of a song, to change the key, and come into it againe, is allowed. Wherefore the names [in other words, the practice of solmization], being the least necessary and most troublesome accident, let this suffice' (sig. Aviii^v).

It may be that Bathe's discussion of the tuning of pitches altered by accidental flats is the most frequently cited passage in his treatise, no doubt on account of the author's provocative yet ambiguous use of the word *key* and his intimations of something apparently akin to modulation. Unfortunately, this is the only mention of these subjects in his treatise. It seems clear that Bathe associates the differing treatment that the singer should give to accidental flats and sharps with distinctly different musical processes that give rise to them, but just what he has in mind he does not say. Owens has examined Bathe's use of these terms in the light of similar ideas expressed by Morley, Campion and other writers, and has compiled from them an analytical vocabulary that promises to refine our understanding of the tonal structure of the music they considered.[93] Through such research, it may be that Bathe's discussion of accidentals, and his intriguing hints at their theoretical origins, will prove to be the most valuable aspect of his pedagogical work for modern music historians.

A numerical method for composing canons

Of no less interest to historians of music theory, however, is the remarkable numerical method for composing canons that appears towards the end of Bathe's book. This method, which is based on a combinatorial algorithm that the student solves repeatedly by use of a numerical table, is intended to enable the beginning musician to compose canons of a kind called 'two parts in one' upon a plainsong. This type of canon, in which two voices are set in strict diatonic imitation above a tenor, was widely popular in Bathe's England, as publications such as Whythorne's *Duos, or Songs for Tvvo Voices* (1590) and John Farmer's *Diuers & Sundry Waies of Two Parts in One* (1592) attest.[94] 'Two parts in one' was also a form that many considered exceedingly difficult both to learn and to teach. A dialogue about the subject in Morley's *A Plaine and Easie Introduction to Practicall Musicke* makes this point dramatically clear. After providing his rhetorical student with a cursory description of such canons, Philomathes, the rhetorical teacher in Morley's text, makes an attempt to depart from the subject without providing any guidance at all about how one may learn to compose in the form. When Philomathes states that 'I will onlie set you downe an example of the most vsual waies [so] that you may by your selfe put them in practise', his student becomes incredulous. 'What?', the student asks, 'Be there no rules to be obserued in the making of two partes in one vppon a plainsong?' To this Philomathes is compelled to reply, with a rare degree of introspection, 'No, verelie, in that the forme of making the Canons is so manie and diuers waies altered, that no generall rule may be gathered.'[95]

As Bathe's text reveals, however, Morley did have at least one peer who had, some years earlier, made a courageous attempt to codify and systematize the teaching of canons of 'two parts in one'. To be sure, there were some on the Continent who appear to have attempted similar feats even earlier; in his 1553 treatise *Introduttione facilissima, et novissima*, the Portuguese composer Vicente Lusitano provided his readers with a comprehensive list of ways in which they could compose short canonic pieces above plainsong tenors of a variety of contours.[96] Yet Bathe's method may provide the most explicit evidence so far discovered that some pre-Baroque composers did in fact rely on the sorts of combinatorial approaches to canonic composition that modern scholars have recently begun to explore.[97] Moreover, the tabular, numerical means that Bathe devised to communicate his method were remarkably forward-looking, anticipating by virtue of both conception and design the sorts of compositional algorithms typically associated with the German Baroque and most famously embodied in the compositional machines designed by the Jesuit writer Athanasius Kircher in the mid-seventeenth century.[98]

In spite of its ambitious origins and novel approach, however, Bathe's method is not without problems. First, his table seems incapable, despite his claims, of teaching the composition of anything other than simple, two-voice canons above a plainsong.[99] Furthermore, his discussion of the use of the table is rendered especially opaque by imprecise and inconsistent punctuation and some particularly unfortunate typographical errors – a situation that could not have been helped by his absence from England at the time of publication. Nonetheless, Bathe's work in this area represents a significant innovation, not followed by later writers. In place of the inductive, trial-and-error methods offered by his contemporaries, Bathe provides his readers with a prescriptive and deductive approach to the problem. In this respect, his work raises some intriguing historiographical questions about the state of theoretical knowledge and analytical practice during his time.

Before the student of Bathe's method can learn to compose settings of two parts in one, he or she must first become familiar with the author's idiosyncratic and rather peculiar use of two terms, *place* and *course*. With respect to the former, Bathe writes: 'First it is to be vnderstanded by this word place, is ment the distance of the following part, to the former part, as the same place or vnison, is called the first place, the next or second place is called the second place, whether it be vp or downe, &c' (sig. Ci[r]). By *place* Bathe means the vertical interval at which imitation occurs between the two canonic voices. If the following part or *comes* begins a perfect fourth above the leading part or *dux* (for instance, if the leading part begins on C and the following part begins on the F above), the *place* is said to be a 'fourth up'. If the leading part were to begin on D and the following part on the C below, the *place* would be said to be a 'second down'. Throughout all settings of 'two parts in one', the *place* remains constant.

Bathe uses the word *course* to describe, in step-by-step fashion, the melodic unfolding of the tenor that underlies the canon. The temporal interval over which the *course* is computed is the same as the temporal displacement between the initial entrances of the two canonic voices. Bathe defines this variable as follows:

> Next heere is to be vnderstanded that by this word, Course, is ment the distaunce of that which followeth iust so long after, as the following part resteth to that which goeth beefore, in the plaine Song or ground[;] as if the following part haue a Semibreefe rest, then the Note of t[h]e ground is in the first course, which hath in the same place that which followeth, iust a Semibreefe length after[;] and that note is in the second course, which hath in the second place that which followeth iust a Semibreefe length after, whether it bee vp or downe, &c. (fol. Ci[r])

Two settings of canons of 'two parts in one', as provided by Morley and shown in Example 6, will serve to illustrate Bathe's use of the terms *place* and *course*; I have indicated the *courses* with slurs. In Example 6a, the following canonic voice enters a perfect fourth above the leading canonic voice. The *place* in this setting is therefore said to be a 'fourth up'. The temporal displacement between the two canonic voices is a semibreve, and so the *courses* of the setting are found by computing the melodic intervals arising between notes a semibreve apart in the tenor. In this case, the first *course* is a 'fourth up', since the distance between G and C, the first two semibreves in the tenor, is a fourth. The second *course* in the setting is a 'second up' – the distance between C and D, the second and third semibreves. The third course is a 'fifth down', the distance between D and G, and so on.

In Example 6b, the following canonic voice, now in the middle of the setting, enters a sixth below the leading voice; the *place* in this setting is therefore said to be a 'sixth down'. The temporal displacement between the two canonic voices is two semibreves apart in the tenor. The first *course* in this case is a 'third up', the distance between G, the first note of the tenor, and B, the note that sounds two semibreves later. The second *course* is a 'third down' – the distance between C, sounding on the second semibreve of the setting, and A, sounding on the fourth. The third *course* is also a 'third down' – the distance between B, sounding on the third semibreve, and G, sounding on the fifth.

Having learnt the meaning of the word *place*, and how to compute all the *courses* of a plainsong, the student is ready to turn to Bathe's table and to begin to compose his or her own settings of 'two parts in one'. Bathe's table is shown in Figure 2.[100]

Example 6 Settings of 'two parts in one' from Morley, *A Plaine and Easie Introduction*: (a) p. 98 (Harman, 180); (b) p. 101 (Harman, 183). Slurs indicate *courses*

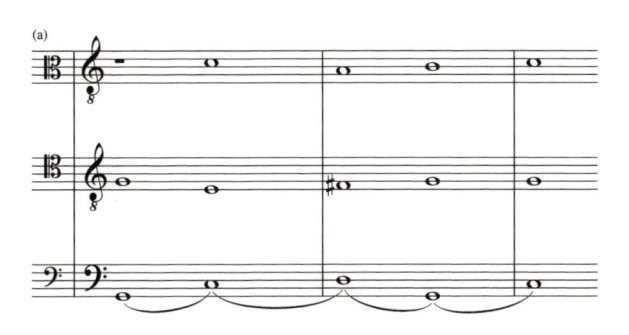

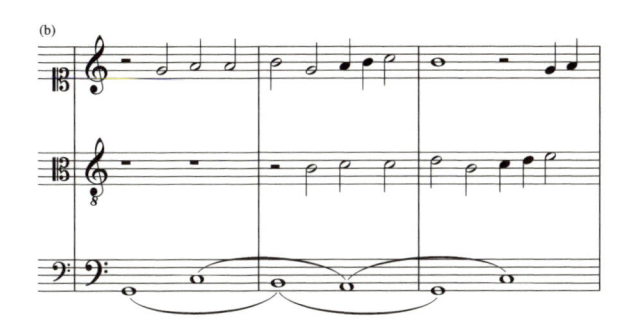

On the left side of the table, in the second row from the top, the student first locates the label 'Places vp' and scans from left to right along that row reading the numbers 1, 7, 6, 5, 4, 3 and 2. The columns in which these numbers stand correspond to the *place* at the unison, the *place* a 'seventh up', the *place* a 'sixth up' and so on. Just below the label 'Places vp', the student finds the labels 'Courses vp' and 'Courses dovvne'. Underneath these labels, he or she finds two columns of the numbers 1 to 8. The rows in which these numbers stand correspond to the *course* a 'second up' or a 'seventh down', the *course* a 'third up' or a 'sixth down' and so on.

In order to compose a setting of 'two parts in one', the student begins by locating the column on the table that corresponds to the *place* at which the imitation is to occur. Since the *place* is constant throughout the setting, he or she remains in this column throughout the rest of the compositional process. Turning to the tenor, he or she then computes, one by one, each *course* of the plainsong. For each *course*, he or she locates the row that corresponds to that *course* on the table, and then moves from left to right

	6	8	11	10	9	8	7	6
The obseruations of the places vp are fixe	5	5	7	6	5	4	3	2
	4	1	6	5	4	3	2	1
	3	7	1	7	6	5	4	3
	2	2	6	7	1	2	3	4
	1	5	2	3	4	5	6	7
	1	1						

Places vp.	1	7	6	5	4	3	2
Courses vp. 1 / Courses downe.	1356	6	135	16	35	136	5
2	7 6	135	16	35	136	5	1356
3	6 135	16	35	136	5	1356	6
4	5 16	35	136	5	1356	6	135
5	4 35	136	5	1356	6	135	36
6	3 136	5	1356	6	135	16	35
7	2 5	1356	6	135	16	35	136
8 vt su: 1	1356	6	135	16	35	136	5
Places down	1	2	3	4	5	6	7

The obseruations of the places down are fixe.	1	1	2	3	4	5	6	7
	2	5	6	7	1	2	3	4
	3	2	3	4	5	6	7	1
	4	7	1	2	3	4	5	6
	5	1	2	3	4	5	6	7
	6	5	6	7	8	9	10	11

Figure 2 'A generall Table comprehending two parts in one, of all kindes vpon all plaine Songs' from Bathe, *A Briefe Introduction to the Skill of Song*, sig. Bviii^v

across that row until it intersects with the column corresponding to the *place*. In the square at which this row and this column intersect, he or she finds all of the intervals at which the leading voice of the canon may be written above the tenor at that particular moment of its unfolding. Bathe describes this process as follows:

> Thus beeing knowne [that is, how to find the *place* and the *course* of a setting], first looke in what place vp or downe, you would haue the following part to bee, which is according to the pleasure of the maker, and so it is how long the following part shall rest. Then looke in what course vp or downe is the note of the ground, for which you would make, then looke what square of the table meeteth with the place and course, and there you shall find noted by figures [numbers], what concord serueth for that course. (sig. Ci^{r-v})

We may now retrace the steps that a student would take when beginning to compose a setting of 'two parts in one' by way of Bathe's method.

Before turning to Bathe's table, the student must make three preliminary decisions: he or she must select a plainsong tenor above which to compose the canon, decide upon the *place* at which imitation is to occur, and decide upon the temporal interval between the initial entrances of the two canonic voices. For the sake of the present discussion, we may assume that the student has selected the plainsong tenor whose beginning is shown in Example 7, that the *place* of the setting will be a 'fifth up', and that one whole note will separate the entrances of the voices.

Example 7   A plainsong tenor (beginning)

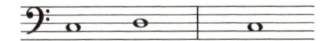

Having made these preliminary decisions, the student can begin to compose. First, he or she computes the first *course* of the plainsong tenor; here, the first *course* is a 'second up'. Next, he or she turns to the table, and locates the row corresponding to this *course* (the fourth row from the top; see Figure 2). Having found this row, the student scans from left to right along the row until it intersects with the column corresponding to the predetermined *place* a 'fifth up' (the fifth column from the left). In the square at which this row and this column intersect, the student finds the numbers 3 and 5. These numbers indicate that he or she may write in the first note of the leading canonic voice at either a third or a fifth above the tenor. As shown in Example 8, our student chooses the third, and thus begins the leading canonic voice with an E.

In order to continue composing his or her setting according to Bathe's method, the student simply repeats all of the steps just taken, only now relative to the second *course* of the tenor. First, the student computes the second *course* of the tenor; here, the second course is a 'second down'. Then,

38   *A Briefe Introduction to the Skill of Song,* Part I

Example 8   Composing a setting of 'two parts in one': beginning

he or she locates the row corresponding to this *course* on the table (the ninth from the top in Figure 2), and scans across this row until it intersects with the columnn corresponding to the unchanging *place* of the setting (the fifth from the left). Finding that the numbers 1, 3 and 5 are contained in the square of intersection, he or she recognizes that the second note of the leading canonic voice can be written at the unison, the third above, or the fifth above the tenor. As shown in Example 9, our student chooses the third, and thus has the leading voice move to an F on the second whole note of the setting.

Example 9   Composing a setting of 'two parts in one': continuation

Continuing in this way until the end of the tenor is reached, the student would, in theory, complete the entire leading voice of the canon without giving any thought to the following voice, yet confident that the following voice is simultaneously being generated in a satisfactory manner.[101] The generation of the following voice is illustrated in Example 10.

As the composer of this setting would have learnt from Bathe's table, there were two pitches on which he or she could begin the leading canonic voice: on the third or the fifth above the tenor. Since the student decided at the start that the *place* would be a 'fifth up', and that a semibreve would separate the initial entrances of the two canonic voices, he or she would know that whatever

Example 10 Generation of the following voice: beginning. Arrow indicates relationship between canonic voices

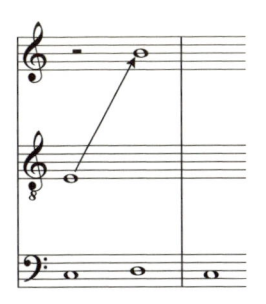

pitch was selected for the leading voice would reappear in the following voice one semibreve later and transposed upward by a fifth. The arrow in Example 10 indicates this relationship. By the time that the first note of the leading voice reappeared transposed as the first note of the following voice, however, the tenor would have already proceeded to its next note, with which the resultant pitch must be consonant. Here, the student has chosen to begin the leading voice on the third above the tenor, E. This note reappears one whole semibreve later in the following part as a B, which is consonant with the tenor at this new point in time, a D. Example 11 shows the outcome of the other choice that Bathe's table provides the student in this instance, as well as the consequence that the student would face if he or she chose instead to break with Bathe's method from the start.

As shown in Example 11a, if the student had chosen to begin the leading canonic voice on the fifth above the tenor rather than the third (a choice for which Bathe's table also provides), the first note of the following voice would have been a D. This resultant pitch D is of course consonant with the tenor at this new point in time, also a D. Example 11b shows the consequence of breaking with Bathe's method from the start. If the student had chosen to begin the leading canonic voice on the note a sixth above the tenor, A (a choice not provided by the table), then this note would reappear one whole note later in the following voice as an E, which would clash with the tenor's D. In this case, any choice for the leading canonic voice other than those provided by Bathe's table will likewise generate a dissonance when transformed into the following voice.[102]

As the student continued to compose the present setting, he or she was alerted by Bathe's table to the fact that three pitches were appropriate for the second note of the leading canonic voice: a unison, a third or a fifth above the tenor. As shown in Example 12, the student in this case chose to continue the leading voice on the third above the tenor, on F, which causes a C to be generated for the second note of the following voice.

Example 11 Other choices for the leading voice: (a) fifth above the tenor (choice provided by Bathe's table); (b) sixth above the tenor (breaking with Bathe's method)

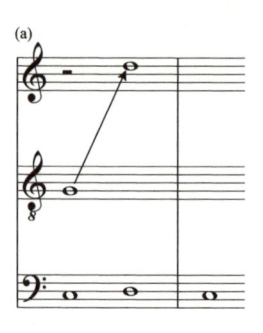

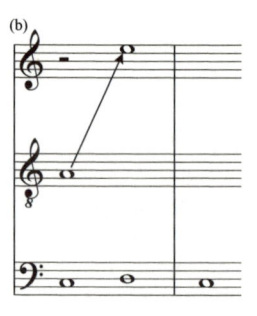

Example 12 Generation of the following voice: continuation

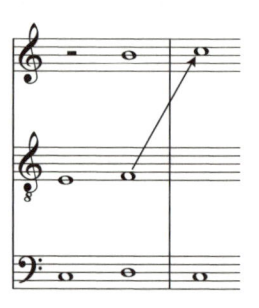

The shortcomings of Bathe's method, however, become apparent as soon as we consider the other options provided by the table in this instance. These options and their results are shown in Example 13. As shown in Example 13a, if the student had chosen to continue the leading canonic voice on D (unison with the tenor), a consonant following voice would have been generated. However, if he or she had instead chosen to continue the leading voice with

Example 13 Other choices provided by Bathe's method: (a) unison with the tenor; (b) fifth above the tenor

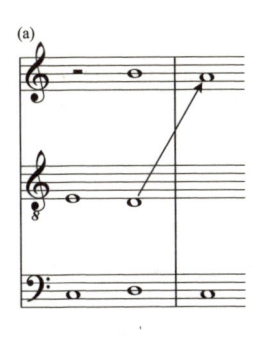

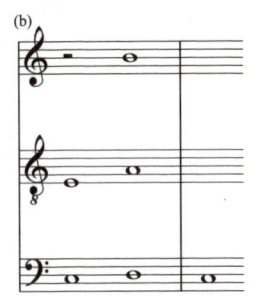

the fifth above the tenor, as shown in Example 13b, he or she would have found that it created a dissonance with the previously generated B in the following voice.

At this point in the compositional process, the student would need to seek additional guidance from a part of Bathe's text entitled 'figures of obseruation' (sig. Ci^v–Cii^r). Here, Bathe provides some cautionary advice to help the student to avoid precisely this kind of voice-leading problem when composing settings of 'two parts in one' at any given *place*. The 'figures of obseruation' themselves are provided on Bathe's table (see Figure 2). In the upper left-hand square of the table, we find the label 'The obseruations of the places vp are sixe: 6 5 4 3 2 1'. In order to find the 'figures of obseruation' for a setting in which the *place* is a 'fifth up', the student locates the column corresponding to that *place* on the table (the fifth from the left), and then looks to the top row of the table to find that the first figure is 4, the second figure is 1, the third figure is 6, and so on. For the meaning of these figures, the student turns to Bathe's discussion on sig. Ci^v–Cii^r. In the setting we have been examining thus far, it is the fourth 'figure of obseruation', 4, that helps us to understand the nature of the problem encountered in Example 13b.

In a setting in which the *place* is a 'fifth up', the third and fourth 'figures of obseruation' are 6 and 4 respectively. With respect to these figures, Bathe writes: 'The third & fourth sheweth what mouing one way with the place, iust so long after as the following part resteth, maketh discords' (sig. Cii[r]). In other words, these figures indicate that, if either a rising melodic sixth or a rising melodic fourth is composed in the leading canonic voice, a dissonance will result between the two canonic voices after a delay equal to the temporal separation of the initial entrances of these voices.[103] As shown in Example 13b, the problematic setting has just such a fourth in the leading canonic voice, E–A. This results, as Bathe's 'figures of obseruation' predict, in a dissonance arising a semibreve later between the two canonic voices. The other 'figures of obseruation' alert the student to similar potential problems. The fifth and sixth 'figures of obseruation' indicate the intervals that must not be used consecutively in the leading canonic voice if consecutive fifths or octaves are to be avoided between the two canonic voices.[104] The significance of the first and second 'figures of obseruation' is uncertain.[105]

Although Bathe assures his readers that they may learn, by means of his method, to compose settings of 'two parts in one' with 'such facilitie, that the vpper part is made, and neuer booked' (sig. Bviii[r]), a careful examination of Example 12 reveals that even mastering the use of his table and studying carefully his 'figures of obseruation' cannot ensure, in themselves, that a correct setting is being created. Upon reconsidering the setting composed in Example 12, the student would probably recognize that the second note of the leading canonic voice, F, makes an augmented, rather than perfect, fourth with the following voice. Bathe's 'figures of obseruation' do not account for such a situation, and he does not clearly address the issue of augmented or diminished intervals in the body of his text. Twice he notes that 'sharp for flat, or flat for sharp, contrary to the order of the place should not bee [written] iust so long after as the following part resteth' (sig. Cii[r]), a statement that seems as though it might address such an issue. Just what he has in mind, however, is far from clear. Immediately after explaining his 'figures of obseruation', Bathe presents an ingenious, abbreviated version of his table depicted in the form of a 'musical sword' (a 'Gladius Musicus') on whose hilt and blade are inscribed poetic verses in which the vowels in each word represent the intervals above the tenor at which one may write in the leading canonic voice.[106] His text concludes without providing his readers with any guidance relating to counterpoint or dissonance treatment.

Conclusion: Bathe's Uncertain Legacy

Given the publication date of his *A Plaine and Easie Introduction to Practicall Musicke* (1597), Morley's claim that he knew of no method for composing canons of 'two parts in one' is understandable. After all, Bathe's *A Briefe Introduction to the Skill of Song* was published only the previous year, and quite possibly after Morley had completed work on his own book. Yet almost 70 years after Bathe's text appeared in print, Christopher Simpson could still write in his *Compendium of Practical Music* (1665) that 'this of which I now speak [that is, canonic composition] cannot be reduced to any rule that I know as depending merely upon sight, and therefore all we can do is only to give you what help or assistance we are able towards the effecting of it'.[107] Turning to the subject of 'two parts in one', Simpson provided his readers with directions that were no more specific than those offered by Morley over six decades earlier. 'First you are to consider what notes will serve your present purpose for the leading part and also suit your following part in reference to the next note of the plainsong,' Simpson advised. 'When you have found out notes that will fit both these occasions, set them down.'[108]

Given the fact that Bathe was hardly an obscure figure in the Elizabethan musical community, it does not seem possible that Simpson, Morley and others were simply unfamiliar with his treatise. We must therefore turn in conclusion to a consideration of the strange lack of reception that Bathe's work seems to have suffered in the hands of his peers. As I hope to have shown over the course of this introduction, Bathe's theories, in spite of the criticisms of Hawkins and others, are in no way confused or inconsistent. Rather, Bathe understood with rare acuity some of the greatest problems faced by both students and teachers in his day, and he was able to propose some truly creative solutions. Some of these solutions, including his four-syllable, non-hexachordal solmization method and the tabular 'compositional machine' that he devised in order to assist in the composition of two-voice canons, were truly forward-looking, and anticipated by years and even decades the sorts of work in these areas that would be pursued by many others. But as a careful examination of his directives for composing canons confirms, Bathe's methods of teaching were often far from perfect, and were quite possibly considered by his contemporaries to offer little real improvement over those that were already widely used in his day.

In the case of his discussion of 'two parts in one', Bathe claimed to offer his readers a method by which they could learn to compose a leading canonic voice without even pausing to consider its transformation into a two-part canonic texture. However, his own 'figures of obseruation' make clear that the application of his method in fact requires a great deal of conscientious checking and rechecking of the polyphonic texture as it unfolds, and a continual adjustment and readjustment of the leading canonic voice as one proceeds. Bathe's approach to the problem that he set out to solve was boldly rationalistic and deductive, and the solution that he devised would have indeed enabled his students to generate a set of compositional possibilities with little effort. Beyond that, however, the task of shaping these possibilities into a satisfactory piece of music would have remained just as inductive and unteachable – in a word, as *artistic* – as ever.

In early 1591, Bathe left England for the Continent and abandoned his early interests in music pedagogy. Nonetheless, his later work as a Jesuit provided him with ample opportunities for teaching, and his pedagogical contributions to a number of other fields have been recognized as every bit as innovative as those that he published in *A Briefe Introduction to the Skill of Song*. Whether working on his 1611 textbook *Ianua linguarum*, among the first tools designed to aid the teaching of foreign languages within a multilingual culture, or later publishing, under the pseudonym Pedro Manrique, his series of guidebooks to spiritual pilgrimage, Bathe remained active as a gifted and creative educator.[109] He would surely have been pleased to know that, through the work of numerous recent scholars, his writings continue to teach us about the subtleties and complexities of the musical culture of which he was a part.

Notes

[1] Throughout the introduction to this volume, all early titles are rendered with standard modern capitalization. On the emergence of a market for instructional textbooks in late sixteenth-century England, see Jessie Ann Owens, 'Concepts of Pitch in English Music Theory, c. 1560–1640', in Cristle Collins Judd (ed.), *Tonal Structures in Early Music* (New York: Garland, 1998), 189, and Jane Flynn, 'A Reconsideration of the Mulliner Book (British Library Add. MS 30513): Music Education in Sixteenth-Century England' (Ph.D. diss., Duke University, 1993), esp. pp. 241–74.

[2] Jeremy L. Smith, *Thomas East and Music Publishing in Renaissance England* (Oxford and New York: Oxford University Press, 2003), 80 and 191 n. 65. I wish to thank Professor Smith for his helpful responses to a number of questions I had concerning East's work. For a summary of the problems that scholars have faced when attempting to establish a publication date for Bathe's treatise, see Owens, 'Concepts of Pitch in English Music Theory', 233–34. Apart from Owens's work, detailed considerations of possible publication dates are offered in Bernarr Rainbow's introduction to the facsimile edition of Bathe's *A Briefe Introduction to the Skill of Song* (Kilkenny: Boethius Press, 1982; repr. Rochester, NY: University of Rochester Press, 1997), 16–17, and Seán P. Ó Mathúna, *William Bathe, S.J., 1564–1614: A Pioneer in Linguistics* (Amsterdam and Philadelphia: John Benjamins Publishing Company, 1986), 175–76.

[3] See Gerald Johnson, 'William Barley, "Publisher & seller of bookes"', *The Library*, ser. 6, vol. 11 (1989), 10–46.

[4] For a list of English-language instructional texts on music published before 1600, see Owens, 'Concepts of Pitch', 190. The three treatises that pre-date those published in 1596–97 are Bathe's *A Briefe Introductione to the True Art of Musicke* (1584), Adrian Le Roy's *A Briefe and Plaine Instruction to Set All Musicke of Eight Divers Tunes in Tableture for the Lute* (c.1574) and P. Delamotte's *A Brief Introduction to the True Art of Music* (1574). Barry Cooper has argued that Delamotte's book, no copies of which are known to survive, was most likely comprised of excerpts translated from earlier treatises

by Continental writers; see Barry Cooper, 'Englische Musiktheorie im 17. und 18. Jahrhundert', in *Entstehung nationaler Traditionen: Frankreich – England* (Geschichte der Musiktheorie, 9; Darmstadt: Wissenschaftliche Buchgesellschaft, 1986), 158.

5   On East's career as a publisher, see Smith, *Thomas East and Music Publishing in Renaissance England.*

6   See Owens, 'Concepts of Pitch', 233 (on Whythorne) and 200–201 (on Morley). In a well-known passage in his treatise, Morley provides a scathing assessment of Barley's *The Pathvvay to Musicke*; see Morley, *A Plaine and Easie Introduction to Practicall Musicke* (London: Peter Short, 1597; facs., Amsterdam and New York: Da Capo Press, 1969), fol. *3ᵛ (Harman, 130–31).

7   Unless otherwise noted, all biographical details supplied in this volume are taken from Ó Mathúna, *William Bathe*, 33–49.

8   East's entry is dated 22 September 1596. See Edward Arber, *A Transcript of the Registers of the Company of Stationers of London, 1554–1640 A.D.* (London: n.p., 1875–94), iii, 71. Smith discusses the advance registration of publications with the Company of Stationers in 'The Hidden Editions of Thomas East', *Notes: The Quarterly Journal of the Music Library Association*, 53, no. 4 (1997), 1086.

9   Cited in Walter McDonald, 'Irish Ecclesiastical Colleges since the Reformation. Salamanca – III', *Irish Ecclesiastical Record*, ser. 2, vol. 10 (1873–74), 524–25. Bathe's novitiate included an extended spiritual retreat, community service, work in a Tournai hospital and months of pilgrimage; see Ó Mathúna, *William Bathe*, 47–49. Although there seems to have been little uniformity in the experiences of Jesuit novices across Europe, their initiation into the Society was invariably intensive. As John W. O'Malley has described, novices at Simancas were required to spend two hours per day in meditation and one in 'examination of conscience', two reciting the Hours and one-half the Rosary, in addition to attending lectures, receiving other sorts of instruction and providing various forms of community service; they were allowed only six hours of sleep per night. See O'Malley, *The First Jesuits* (Cambridge, Mass.: Harvard University Press, 1993), 361–62.

10   The bulk of the extant text of Bathe's *A Briefe Introductione to the True Art of Musicke* is preserved on fols 41ʳ–52ʳ of University of Aberdeen Library MS 28. A description and transcription of this source, along with a complete list of the portions of the 1584 treatise that were reprinted in *A Briefe Introduction to the Skill of Song*, is provided in Part III of this volume.

11   Unless otherwise noted, all references to Bathe's *A Briefe Introductione to the True Art of Musicke* are to the portion of the text preserved in University of Aberdeen Library MS 28.

12   Sir John Hawkins, *A General History of the Science and Practice of Music* (London, 1776; repr. London: J. Alfred Novello, 1853), 497. The portion of Bathe's *A Briefe Introductione to the True Art of Musicke* preserved in University of Aberdeen Library MS 28 includes the title page but omits the publisher's imprint and preface (both of which are cited by Hawkins).

13   See Ó Mathúna, *William Bathe*, 33–49. Several brief seventeenth-century records of Bathe's activities also survive. These include, in addition to Paul Sherlock's account, a short biographical essay by the Jesuit historian Mathias Tanner, recorded in *Societatis Jesu Europae* (1694) and reprinted in Timothy Corcoran, *Studies in the History of Classical Teaching: Irish and Continental, 1500–1700* (Boston: Benziger Brothers, 1911), 249–54; and a cursory account of Bathe's life and work made by the early historian of Oxford University Anthony Wood, in *Athenae Oxonienses. An Exact History of All the Writers and Bishops Who Have Had Their Education in the Most Ancient and Famous University of Oxford, from the Fifteenth Year of King Henry the*

Seventh, Dom. 1500, to the End of the Year 1690 (London: Thomas Bennet, 1691), i, 335–36.

14   This statement is reprinted in Ó Mathúna, *William Bathe*, 33.

15   On Bathe, Wood writes: 'whether in any of the three houses wherein *Irish* men of this time studied, viz. in *Univ*. coll. *Hart*, or *Glocester*-hall, or whether he took a degree, I find not'; see Wood, *Athenae Oxonienses*, i, 335.

16   See Ó Mathúna, *William Bathe*, 38; and Corcoran, *Studies in the History of Classical Teaching*, 5–6. Along these lines, McDonald has documented the professional, financial and even corporal consequences faced by Irish Catholics who refused to take such oaths as required by their professions during this period. He writes that one 'Andrew Carrol, being chosen mayor, was asked to take the oath of allegiance and supremacy, and on refusing, was cast into prison, and had to pay £100 to an Englishman who had acted for him'; see McDonald, 'Irish Ecclesiastical Colleges since the Reformation', 520.

17   As Owens suggests, it is quite possible that Bathe participated in the masques and other musical activities that played an important part in the social life at Gray's and other Inns; see Owens, 'Concepts of Pitch', 191. On these activities, see Robert W. Wienpahl, *Music at the Inns of Court during the Reigns of Elizabeth, James, and Charles* (Ann Arbor: University Microfilms International, 1979).

18   Although they do not mention Bathe, a pair of recent studies examine this corner of Irish political history in detail and provide a sense of the sort of activities in which Bathe may have been engaged during this period. See Steven G. Ellis, *Ireland in the Age of the Tudors, 1447–1603* (London and New York: Longman, 1998), 318–28, and Ciaran Brady, *The Chief Governors: The Rise and Fall of Reform Government in Tudor Ireland, 1536–1588* (Cambridge: Cambridge University Press, 1994), 291–300.

19   For a discussion of various aspects of the music tutor's work in Elizabethan England, as well as analyses of the social and economic circumstances that gave rise to the rapid expansion of this profession around the turn of the seventeenth century, see David C. Price, *Patrons and Musicians of the English Renaissance* (Cambridge: Cambridge University Press, 1981), 39–47, and John Caldwell, *The Oxford History of English Music* (Oxford: Clarendon Press, 1991), i. 324.

20   On one particularly rich class of such books, the manuals for gentlemanly behaviour, see David Castronovo, *The English Gentleman: Images and Ideals in Literature and Society* (New York: Ungar, 1987) and Philip Mason, *The English Gentleman: The Rise and Fall of an Ideal* (New York: William Morrow, 1982). For more specific considerations of the treatment of music performance and education in these texts, see Price, *Patrons and Musicians in the English Renaissance*, 1–9; Wienpahl, *Music at the Inns of Court*, 65–93; and Susan Hankey, 'The Compleat Gentleman's Music', *Music & Letters*, 62 (1981), 146–54.

21   Referring to such texts in his autobiography, Whythorne observed, 'those books the nobility and the worshipful do much follow in these days'; see *The Autobiography of Thomas Whythorne*, ed. James M. Osborn (London: Oxford University Press, 1962), 205.

22   Elyot's text was first published in London by T. Berthelet in 1531, and was reprinted in 1537, 1544, 1546, 1553, 1557, 1565 and 1580. Hoby's translation of Castiglione's text was first published in London in 1561 by William Seres, and was reprinted in 1584, 1588 and 1603.

23   *The Institucion of a Gentleman* (London: Thomas Marshe, 1555; facs. Amsterdam and Norwood, NJ: Walter J. Johnson, 1974), sig. Bvii^{r-v}.

24   Sir Thomas Elyot, *The Book Named the Governor*, ed. S.E. Lehmberg (New York: Dutton, 1962), 22.

25   Baldassare Castiglione, *The Courtyer* (London: J.M. Dent and Sons, 1974), 100.
26   Henry Peacham, *The Compleat Gentleman* (London: Francis Constable, 1622; facs. Amsterdam and New York: Da Capo Press, 1968), 98–99.
27   See the account of Whythorne's initial encounter with the 'Suds-of-Soap Widow' in *The Autobiography of Thomas Whythorne*, 28.
28   Owens, 'Concepts of Pitch', 234; on these psalms, see Nicholas Temperley, *The Hymn Tune Index: A Census of English-Language Hymn Tunes in Printed Sources from 1535 to 1820* (Oxford: Clarendon Press, 1998), i, 197 (tunes 184a and 250b).
29   Nicholas Temperley, *Music of the English Parish Church* (Cambridge: Cambridge University Press, 1979), i, 71–73. Earlier harmonized psalm collections, none of which is complete with respect to the Psalms of David, include *The whole psalmes in foure partes* (London: John Day, 1563) [*STC* 2431]; William Hunnis, *Seuen Sobs of a Sorrowfull Soule for Sinne* (London: Henry Denham, 1583) [*STC* 13975]; John Cosyn, *Musike of Six, and Fiue Partes* (London: John Wolfe, 1585) [*STC* 5828]; and William Daman, *The Musicke of M. William Damon* (London: Thomas East, 1591) [*STC* 6220–21].
30   Donald W. Krummel, *English Music Printing, 1553–1700* (London: The Bibliographical Society, 1975), 20. For a detailed consideration of 'the politics of the music patents', including the 'psalm-book patent' held by Richard Day, see Krummel's discussion on pp. 10–33.
31   Jeremy L. Smith, 'From "Rights to Copy" to the "Bibliographic Ego": A New Look at the Last Early Edition of Byrd's "Psalmes, Sonets & Songs"', *Music & Letters*, 80 (1999), 521–22.
32   Originally published in 1592 [*STC* 2483], East's psalter was reprinted in 1594 [*STC* 2488], 1604 [*STC* 2514] and 1607 [*STC* 2522.3].
33   *The Whole Booke of Psalmes: With Their Wonted Tunes* (London: Thomas East, 1592) [*STC* 2483], sig. Bi^r.
34   Ó Mathúna has suggested that Bathe may have proceeded directly to Belgium after the conclusion of his diplomatic mission to Spain, undertaken towards the end of 1591; see Ó Mathúna, *William Bathe*, 46.
35   Owens notes that the pages in question 'seem more like appendices than a coherent exposition'; see Owens, 'Concepts of Pitch', 233.
36   For instance, in explaining the use of his table for canonic composition, Bathe remarks: 'Neuerthelesse, they [dissonant intervals] may be brought in, when they may be garded by the place next adioyning, for whatsoeuer maketh a discord, the next place to it maketh a concord' (sig. Ci^v).
37   In *The Pathvvay to Musicke* (London: William Barley, 1596) [*STC* 19464], the list of consonant intervals appears on sig. Fi^r; the discussion of descant in general begins on the preceding page. In Morley's *A Plaine and Easie Introduction*, consonance and dissonance are discussed on pp. 70–71 (Harman, 141–42), at the very beginning of the section entitled 'treating of descant' that commences on p. 69 (Harman, 139). In *A Briefe Introductione to the True Art of Musicke*, Bathe's list of consonant intervals appears on fol. 46^r (in University of Aberdeen Library MS 28); his discussion of counterpoint begins on fol. 50^r.
38   Smith, 'The Hidden Editions of Thomas East', 1070.
39   This situation is discussed by Smith in 'From "Rights to Copy" to the "Bibliographic Ego"', 521–22.
40   There is evidence that East may have engaged in such enterprising and self-promoting activities on other occasions as well. As C.W.R.D. Moseley has suggested, East may have sponsored the production of a play based on one of his own best-selling publications, *Mandeville's Travels*, in the early 1590s. Here too, as in the case

of his psalter, it seems that East sought to promote one of his previously successful publications in a newly published (or staged) form. See Moseley, 'The Lost Play of Mandeville', *The Library*, ser. 5, vol. 25 (1970), 46–49. I am grateful to Jeremy L. Smith for bringing the Mandeville case and Moseley's essay to my attention.

41   Arber, *A Transcript of the Registers of the Company of Stationers*, iii. 95.

42   As Smith observes, 'it was ... standard practice among authors of that era to release any former interest in a volume to its publisher before, or soon after, the first edition appeared in print' (Smith, 'From "Rights to Copy" to the "Bibliographic Ego"', 527). Similarly, Krummel has observed that 'the author (or the composer, or the creator) had no rights, unless he happened to be either the grantee or a stationer'; see Krummel, *English Music Printing*, 10.

43   Smith, 'The Hidden Editions of Thomas East'.

44   Miriam Miller and Jeremy L. Smith, 'Thomas East', in *NG II*, vii. 837.

45   Krummel, *English Music Printing*, 162.

46   See Arber, *A Transcript of the Registers of the Company of Stationers*, ii. 825.

47   Smith, 'The Hidden Editions of Thomas East', 1078.

48   A similar argument has been made by H.K. Andrews relative to East's publication of William Byrd's *Psalmes, Sonets & Songs*; Smith has recently amended Andrews's theory to take account of recent typographical discoveries, yet his essential argument remains intact. See Smith, 'From "Rights to Copy" to the "Bibliographic Ego"', 519–27.

49   See Smith, 'The Hidden Editions of Thomas East', 1086.

50   Smith notes the possibility of competition between East and Morley with regard to these treatises in *Thomas East and Music Publishing in Renaissance England*, 80.

51   Owens, 'Concepts of Pitch', 192 n. 44.

52   Hawkins, *A General History of the Science and Practice of Music*, 497.

53   Ibid., 498.

54   Ibid.

55   For instance, Rebecca Herissone has recently written that 'Several theorists also demonstrated themselves to have misunderstood various principles of the [hexachordal] system, none more so than Bathe who, despite encouraging modernization of pitch organization through the adoption of the seven-note scale, made several abortive attempts to explain aspects of hexachordal theory. He tried and failed to describe a hexachordal rule allowing the interval of a tone to be changed into a semitone where certain melodic figures occurred; and he was also unable to solmize correctly a number of melodies requiring mutation into ficta hexachords.' Herissone, *Music Theory in Seventeenth-Century England* (Oxford: Oxford University Press, 2000), 78–79.

56   The relationship between the appearance, content and intended function of texts produced by the Nuremberg circle of teachers has recently been explored by Cristle Collins Judd in *Reading Renaissance Music Theory: Hearing with the Eyes* (Cambridge: Cambridge University Press, 2000), 82–114.

57   Along these lines, Jane Flynn has argued that Morley's *Plaine and Easie Introduction* does not seem to provide a record of standard instructional practices in the grammar schools of Elizabethan England, as has often been assumed. See Flynn, 'A Reconsideration of the Mulliner Book', 116–17.

58   Facs. in Bernarr Rainbow, *English Psalmody Prefaces: Popular Methods of Teaching, 1562–1835* (Kilkenny: Boethius Press, 1982), 28. The didactic prefaces occur, for example, in *STC* 2430 (facs. in Rainbow, *English Psalmody Prefaces*; reference in Temperley, *The Hymn Tune Index*: *P E4 1562 e); *STC* 2433 (Temperley: *P E7 1564 e); *STC* 2442.5 (Temperley: *P E14 b 1572); and *STC* 2456.4 (Temperley: *P E21 b 1580).

59 Morley, *A Plaine and Easie Introduction to Practicall Musicke*, sig. B1^{r-v} (Harman, 6).
60 Ibid., sig. B1^v (Harman, 7).
61 Thomas Robinson, *The Schoole of Musicke* (London: Thomas East, 1603; facs. Amsterdam and New York: Da Capo Press, 1973), sig. B1^v.
62 On this rhetorical strategy, see, for instance, Richarde Sherrye, *A Treatise of the Figures of Grammer and Rhetorike* (London: Ricardi Totteli, 1555) [*STC* 22429], fol. xxxix^r; Richard Rainolde, *A Booke Called the Foundacion of Rhetorike* (London: John Kingston, 1563) [*STC* 20604], fol. liiii^{r-v}; Thomas Wilson, *The Arte of Rhetorike* (London: John Kingston, 1563) [*STC* 25802], fol. 4^{r-v}; and Abraham Fraunce, *The Arcadian Rhetorike* (London: Thomas Orwin, 1588) [*STC* 11338], fol. H3^{r-v}. Bathe's use of the rhetorical strategy of *objection and answer* was not confined to *A Briefe Introduction to the Skill of Song*; it is employed in his 1584 treatise *A Briefe Introductione to the True Art of Musicke* as well. The extant text of the 1584 treatise is transcribed in Part III of this volume.
63 Sherrye, *A Treatise of the Figures of Grammer and Rhetorike*, fol. xxxix^r.
64 Examples can be found in a pair of theoretical treatises written in the mid-sixteenth century by the Lüneburg teachers Lucas Lossius and Auctor Lampadius. In his *Erotemata musicae practicae* (Nuremberg: Berg and Neuber, 1563), Lossius writes:

> *Quid est Musica?* Musica, est benè, ac modulatè canendi scientia.
> *Quotuplex est Musica?* Duplex, Theorica, & Practica … (sig. A5^r)

> [*What is music?* Music is the science of properly and artfully setting sound in motion.
> *How many kinds of music are there?* Two: theoretical and practical …]

Similarly, Lampadius writes in his *Compendium musices* (Bern: Mathias Apiarius, 1541):

> Quot modis Claues componuntur? Duobus, ex literis & syllabis.
> Quot literis? septe*m*, vt, a, b, c, d, e, f, G … (sig. B3^r)

> [Of how many parts are notes comprised? Two: letters and syllables.
> How many letters? Seven: A, B, C, D, E, F, G …]

65 Lodowick Bryskett, *A Discourse of Civill Life: Containing the Ethike Part of Morall Philosophie* (London: Edward Blount, 1606; facs. Amsterdam and New York: Da Capo Press, 1971), 151–52.
66 The authorship of this book is considered in J.W. Binns, 'John Case and the "Praise of musicke"', *Music & Letters*, 55 (1974), 444–53.
67 *The Praise of Musicke* (Oxford: Joseph Barnes, 1586; facs. Hildesheim and New York: Georg Olms, 1980), 139.
68 On Bathe's method for tuning accidental sharps, see pp. 30–31 in this volume.
69 Wilson, *The Arte of Rhetorike*, fol. 96^r.
70 The theoretical arguments that Bathe presents are considered on pp. 31–32 below.
71 For a detailed comparison of Bathe's solmization method with those described by his late sixteenth- and early seventeenth-century peers, see Owens, 'Concepts of Pitch', 191–215.
72 On the relationship between the *Post-Predicaments* and the rest of the *Categories*, see the essays 'Aristotle' and 'Categories' by, respectively, G.B. Kerferd and Manley

Thompson in *The Encyclopedia of Philosophy*, ed. Paul Edwards (New York and London: Collier and Macmillan, 1967). I wish to thank Professor Jeremiah Hackett for answering several questions on this subject.

[73] As Morley writes, 'When I had ended my booke, and showne it (to be perused) to some of better skill in letters then my selfe, I was by the[m] requested, to giue some contentment to the learned, both by setting down a reason why I had disagreed from the opinions of others, as also to explaine something, which in the booke it selfe might seeme obscure. I haue therefore thought it best to set downe in Annotations, such things as in the text could not so commodiouslie be handled, for interrupting of the continuall course of the matter, that both the young beginner shoulde not be ouerladed with those things, which at the firste woulde be to hard for him to conceiue: and also that they who were more skilful, might haue a reason for my proceedings.' Morley, *A Plaine and Easie Introduction to Practicall Musicke*, sig. ¶1^r (Harman, 100).

[74] For general discussions of the practice of solmization, see Andrew Hughes and Edith Gerson-Kiwi, 'Solmization', in *NG II*, xxiii. 644–53; and Martin Ruhnke, 'Solmisation', in *MGG*, Sachteil, viii. 1561–69.

[75] Bathe, *A Briefe Introductione to the True Art of Musicke*, fol. 43^r.

[76] Important studies of the hexachordal system of solmization include Karol Berger, *Musica ficta: Theories of Accidental Inflections in Vocal Polyphony from Marchetto da Padova to Gioseffo Zarlino* (Cambridge: Cambridge University Press, 1987); Margaret Bent, 'Diatonic Ficta', *Early Music History*, 4 (1984), 1–48; Gaston G. Allaire, *The Theory of Hexachords, Solmization and the Modal System* (n.p.: American Institute of Musicology, 1972); Bent, 'Musica Recta and Musica Ficta', *Musica Disciplina*, 26 (1972), 73–100; Robert V. Henderson, 'Solmization Syllables in Musical Theory, 1100–1600' (Ph.D. diss., Columbia University, 1969); and Eberhard Preußner, 'Solmisationsmethoden im Schulenunterricht des 16. und 17. Jahrhunderts', in Hans Hoffmann and Franz Rühlmann (eds), *Festschrift Fritz Stein zum 60. Geburtstag* (Braunschweig: H. Litolff, 1939), 112–28. For more recent overviews of various aspects of the subject, see Margaret Bent and Alexander Silbiger, 'Musica ficta', in *NG II*, xvii. 441–53; Jehoash Hirshberg, 'Hexachord', in *NG II*, xi. 472–74; Andrew Hughes and Edith Gerson-Kiwi, 'Solmization', in *NG II*, xxiii. 644–53; Christian Berger and Jeffrey J. Dean, 'Hexachord', in *MGG*, Sachteil, iv, 279–92; Martin Ruhnke, 'Solmisation', in *MGG*, Sachteil, viii, 1561–69; and Peter W. Urquhart, 'Musica ficta', in *MGG*, Sachteil, vi, 662–80.

[77] Lossius, *Erotemata musicae practicae*, sigs. B8^v–C1^v.

[78] The solmization systems of Morley, Bathe and other English writers are discussed in Owens, 'Concepts of Pitch', 191–215; Herissone, *Music Theory in Seventeenth-Century England*, 74–91; Timothy A. Johnson, 'Solmization in the English Treatises around the Turn of the Seventeenth Century: A Break from Modal Theory', *Theoria*, 5 (1990–91), 42–60; and Barry Cooper, 'Englische Musiktheorie im 17. und 18. Jahrhundert', 184–86.

[79] 'Euery Note in the order of Ascension is a whole note or tone aboue the next vnder, saue the vpper & nether Fa, which be but halfe notes or Semitones' (sig. Biii^{r-v}).

[80] See Thomas Campion, *A New Way of Making Fowre Parts in Counter-Point*, ed. Christopher R. Wilson (Aldershot and Burlington, VT: Ashgate, 2003), 44–45. Campion's solmization system is discussed in Owens, 'Concepts of Pitch', 208–11; Johnson, 'Solmization in the English Treatises', 53–57; Cooper, 'Englische Musiktheorie', 184–86; and Ernst Apfel, *Geschichte der Kompositionslehre: Von den Anfängen bis gegen 1700* (Wilhelmshaven: Heinrichshofen's Verlag, 1981), 601–3.

[81] See Owens, 'Concepts of Pitch', 191–97, and Johnson, 'Solmization in the English Treatises', 43–48.
[82] Sebald Heyden, *De arte canendi*, trans. Clement A. Miller (n.p.: American Institute of Musicology, 1972), 36–37.
[83] Cooper suggests, however, that English theorists may have inherited the idea that the lowered seventh degree is an inherent part of the octave scale at least in part from Continental writers, who, by the mid-sixteenth century, generally allowed the singer to name this pitch *fa* without mutation provided that the notes on either side of it were the sixth degree (*la*) of a single hexachord; see Cooper, 'Englische Musiktheorie', 184–85. The theoretical implications of this common allowance within the hexachordal system, often known by the verse *una nota super la semper est canendum fa*, have been explored by Bent in 'Diatonic Ficta', 11–12, and 'Musica Recta and Musica Ficta', 92. The historical origins of this practice are examined in Allaire, *The Theory of Hexachords, Solmization and the Modal System*, 45–47.
[84] See Owens, 'Concepts of Pitch'; she provides a tabular summary of such collections on p. 230.
[85] On the history and characteristics of solfège type, see Krummel, *English Music Printing*, 71–73. In a preliminary study of the music contained in Day's *The Whole Booke of Psalmes*, I have found solfège type used in 10 out of 31 pre-1600 copies examined. These editions were printed in 1569 [*STC* 2439.5], 1572 (facs. in Rainbow, *English Psalmody Prefaces*, 40–41), 1573 [*STC* 2443], 1576 [*STC* 2446, 2447], 1578 [*STC* 2449.7], 1583 (in private collection), 1588 [*STC* 2475] and 1600 [*STC* 2500, 2500.3].
[86] Facs. in Rainbow, *English Psalmody Prefaces*, 40.
[87] See Owens, 'Concepts of Pitch', 201–2.
[88] This process has been described previously in Owens, 'Concepts of Pitch', 198–99.
[89] In terms of the mental process involved, the technique would be similar (albeit in this respect only) to what Johannes Cochlaeus called 'mental mutation'. He wrote: 'What is mental mutation? It means to sing one vocable and to keep the other in mind. This kind of mutation is more suitable than the prior kind ['explicit mutation', that is, pronouncing two syllables on the pivotal pitch on which a mutation occurs], for singing both syllables means singing the same note twice, which is neither pleasing to the ears nor fitting in a song. Moreover, in mensural music it is completely intolerable, especially in smaller note values in which the speed of the notes does not allow a repetition of the same note. Thus explicit mutation is considered only as a beginning, but implicit mutation is its continuation and practical application.' Cochlaeus, *Tetrachordum musices*, trans. Clement A. Miller (n.p.: American Institute of Musicology, 1970), 43. The idea of mental mutation is discussed in Berger, *Musica ficta*, 7.
[90] This example is also transcribed and discussed in Owens, 'Concepts of Pitch', 199.
[91] See ibid., 198–99.
[92] Jeffrey Dean has recently suggested that the lack of effect that accidental sharps seem to have had upon solmization is characteristic of the fifteenth-century discourse on hexachordal theory as a whole; see Berger and Dean, 'Hexachord', 287. Although Morley does not explicitly address the problem of tuning sharps in his treatise, he includes one example of solmization that includes a cadential F♯; the syllables that he assigns to the notes in this passage indicate that the appearance of the sharp does not affect the solmization. See Morley, *A Plaine and Easie Introduction to Practicall Musicke*, 9 (Harman, 18).

93 Owens, 'Concepts of Pitch'.
94 Whythorne, *Duos, or Songs for Tvvo Voices* (London: Thomas East, 1590) [*STC* 25583]; John Farmer, *Diuers & Sundry Waies of Two Parts in One, to the Number of Fortie, vppon One Playnsong* (London: Thomas East, 1591) [*STC* 10698]. As Elway Bevin's *A Briefe and Short Instruction of the Art of Musicke* (London: R. Young, 1635) attests, the form remained popular nearly a half-century after Bathe completed work on his volume (see pp. 7–19 in Bevin's text). For a general consideration of 'two parts in one', see Hugh Milton Miller, 'Forty Wayes of 2 Pts. in One of Tho[mas] Woodson', *Journal of the American Musicological Society*, 8 (1955), 14–21. As Jane Flynn has noted, studying this and other types of canon was believed by many late sixteenth-century musicians to be an especially valuable pedagogical exercise; see Flynn, 'A Reconsideration of the Mulliner Book', 259–63, and 'The Education of Choristers in England during the Sixteenth Century', in John Morehen (ed.), *English Choral Practice, 1400–1650* (Cambridge: Cambridge University Press, 1995), 195.
95 Morley, *A Plaine and Easie Introduction to Practicall Musicke*, 98 (Harman, 180).
96 Vincente Lusitano, *Introduttione facilissima, et novissima, di canto fermo, figurato, contraponto semplice, et in concerto* (Venice: Francesco Rampazetto; facs. Rome: Libreria musicale italiana, 1989), fols 17^r–21^v. I wish to thank Professors Julie Cumming and Susan Weiss for bringing Lusitano's work in this area to my attention.
97 See Alan Gosman, 'Stacked Canon and Renaissance Compositional Procedure', *Journal of Music Theory*, 41 (1997), 289–317.
98 See Kircher, *Musurgia universalis*, ii (Rome: Ludovico Grignani, 1650; facs. Hildesheim and New York: Georg Olms 1970), 185–90. Much of the second volume of Kircher's treatise is concerned with combinatorial methods for composing in various forms and styles; see, for instance, his method for composing canons at the unison on pp. 165–66. Kircher's machines are discussed in detail in Claudio Annibaldi, 'Froberger in Rome: From Frescobaldi's Craftsmanship to Kircher's Compositional Secrets', *Current Musicology*, 58 (1995), 5–27, and 'La macchina dei cinque stili: nuovi documenti sul secondo soggiorno romano di Johann Jakob Froberger', in *La musica a Roma attraverso le fonti d'archivio. Atti del Convegno internazionale Roma 4–7 giugno 1992*, ed. Bianca Maria Antolini, Arnaldo Morelli and Vera Vita Spagnuolo (Lucca: Libreria musicale italiana, 1994), 399–408. I am grateful to Professor Jessie Ann Owens for bringing Kircher's work in this area to my attention.
99 Bathe's assertion that 'This present table, may serue also, who so marketh it well, for 2 parts in one, without a plaine song, of all kinds, & in all waies for 3 parts in one, without a plainsong, or ground, the third part being vnder: of all kindes & of all wayes for 2 parts in one, vpon 2 plain songs, or grou[n]ds at once, for maintaining reports, & other such things as these be' (sig. Ci^r) does not seem to be borne out by the method described in his text.
100 Some observations on Bathe's tabular mode of representing his material have been made in Joseph Ortiz, 'Musical Alphabets: *Musica speculativa* and the (Mis)representation of Sound in Early Modern England', paper read at the annual meeting of the Renaissance Society of America, April 2002, Scotsdale, Arizona.
101 The intervals shown in the square of intersection are all of those that will not produce seconds, fourths or sevenths when augmented by the *place* and diminished by the *course*. This algorithm assumes that the interval between the leading voice and the tenor, when transposed upward or downward by the *place* and adjusted to take account of the *course* (that is, when transformed into the interval between the *following* voice and the tenor), will not be a harmonic dissonance – a second, fourth or seventh.

[102] Unfortunately, Bathe's discussion of this point includes a potentially disorienting error. On sig. Ci^v of his treatise, we read that 'All Concords next expressed in the square, make discords betwixt the vpper part and the plaine song or ground'; in the case of the present example, this would imply that the fifth above the tenor, rather than any interval *but* the fifth or third, will generate a dissonant following ('vpper') voice. As Example 10 (among others) makes clear, *all* intervals shown in the square of intersection generate a following canonic voice that is consonant with the tenor. Those intervals that are *not* shown in the square are those that generate dissonances. The beginning of Bathe's passage should therefore read 'All Concords *not* expressed in the square'; the corrected text has been noted in the present edition.

[103] These intervals will result in a leading voice that is a second above or below the following voice. The algorithm may be expressed as follows:

third 'figure of obseruation' minus *place* = 2nd
fourth 'figure of obseruation' minus *place* = 7th

[104] The algorithm may be expressed as follows:

fifth 'figure of obseruation' minus *place* = unison (or 8ve)
sixth 'figure of obseruation' minus *place* = 5th

[105] The algorithm may be expressed as follows:

first 'figure of obseruation' plus *place* = 8ve
second 'figure of obseruation' plus *place* = 5th

[106] The use of the 'musical sword' is described in the Explanatory Notes accompanying Bathe's treatise in Part II of this volume.

[107] Christopher Simpson, *A Compendium of Practical Music in Five Parts*, ed. Phillip J. Lord (Oxford: Basic Blackwell, 1970), 94.

[108] Ibid., 95.

[109] On these aspects of Bathe's work, see Ó Mathúna, *William Bathe*.

PART II

William Bathe,
A Briefe Introduction to the Skill of Song

Editorial Note

Eight copies of Bathe's treatise are known to exist at present: two in the British Library, London (one incomplete; facsimile edition of the complete exemplar by Bernarr Rainbow); and one each at Sion College, the Bodleian Library of Oxford University, Cambridge University Library, the Dublin Public Library, the Houghton Library of Harvard University, and the William Andrews Clark Memorial Library of the University of California at Los Angeles. The copy text for the present edition is the facsimile edition of the complete British Library exemplar. The copies owned by the Cambridge University Library, Harvard University, and the University of California at Los Angeles were also consulted; no discrepancies between these copies were detected.

In keeping with the aims of the series, this edition presents the original text, retaining punctuation, spelling and capitalization. There are three exceptions: the modern form of the letter 's' has been used throughout; where the original lacked a space between two adjacent words, a space has been added tacitly; where a tilde appears over a letter in the original, indicating the need to supply an 'm' or an 'n' immediately afterwards, the missing 'm' or 'n' is supplied in italics. Wherever possible, the formatting of the original print has also been maintained. Corrections to the original text are given as footnotes. Explanatory notes relating to Bathe's discussion are provided as endnotes to the edition.

Edition

[sig. Ai^r]

A BRIEFE INTRO-
duction to the skill of
SONG:

Concerning the practise, set forth by William Bathe

Gentleman.

In which work is set downe X. sundry wayes of 2. parts in one vpon the plaine song. Also a Table newly added of the comparisons of Cleues, how one followeth another for the naming of Notes: with other necessarie examples, to further the learner.

FABIVS.

Musica est honestum et iucundum oblectamentum, liberalibus ingenijs maxime dignum.[1]

LONDON
Printed by Thomas Este.

58   *A Briefe Introduction to the Skill of Song,* Part II

[sig. Aii^r]
To the Reader.

IGnorance as Diuines doe testifie, is one of the plagues put vpon man the creature, for transgressing of the commaundements of God his creatour, from which we are to come, (as the patient from his disease) by degrees. Mans vnderstanding is likened by Aristotle to the eies of the Howlet in the day-light. Salomon sayth: Dedi cor meum vt scirem prudentiam, doctrinam, erroresq;, et stultitiam, et agnoui quod in his quoq; est labor et atflictio spiritus.[2]

The fame of our ancestours that diligently laboured to bring vs, and in many things brought vs, from ignorance to knowledge, shall neuer be forgotten so long as those things wherein they laboured, be in estimation, and (in mine opinion) so farre forth as we may, we should Imitate the steps of them, for this plague of ignorance is so great, that neither did they, neither shall we finde so much: but that we must leaue sufficient, for our posteritie to be found.

Wherefore seeing sufficiently others to labour and trauell in other Sciences, I thought good to bestow my labour in Musicke, seeing that paines might so much preuaile, as by the fruit of my labour may plainly appeare. I tooke the matter in hand vpon this occasion, though it were far distant from my profession, being desired by a gentleman, to instruct him in song, I gaue him such rules as my Master gaue mee: Yet could I giue him no song so plaine, wherein there chanced not some one thing or other, to which none of those rules could directly leade him. Marking then how in minde, I did know what by rule I could not teach, I perceiued how [sig. Aii^v] *vnder the shade of rule, I attained to many things by rote: and how pleasant, speedie and sure it is to runne by rule, I tooke this labour in hand, and brought it to this passe. Olde Musitions laid downe for Song, manifold and crabbed, confuse,*[a] *tedious rules, as for example: though there be in all but six names, Vt, Re, Me, Fa, Sol, La, hauing amongst them an easie order, yet could not they by rule declare, whether of these should bee attributed to euery Note, vnlesse they had first framed the long ladder or skale of Gam-vt, to which some added, thinking the ladder too short, some hewed off a peece, thinking it too long. Then would they haue the learner be as perfect in comming downe backward, as in going vp forward, least in his practise he should fall, and breake his neck. Then must he learne, Gam-vt in rule, Are, in space, b my in rule, C faut in space, &c. Then must he know Gam vt, how many cleues, how many notes. Are, how many notes, &c. Then must he know b, quadrij, proper chant and bemul, re in Are, whereby vt in Cfaut, whereby mi, in Alamire, whereby &c. And when all haue done, after their long circumstances of time, whereby they should be often driuen to millibi,*[b] *for Notes standing in diuerse places of Gam-vt, haue names that the place where they stand*

---

[a] Should read *confused.*
[b] Should read *nullibi.*

comprehend not. Touching all the prolixe circumstances, & needlesse difficulties, that they vse, it loathes me greatly that heere I should write them: & much more would it grieue the Reader to learne them. Also many things are vsed in Song, for which they giue no rules at all, but committed them to dodge at it, harke to it, aud[c] harpe vpon it. Now (Reader) th'effect of my pretended purpose, and fruit of my finished labor is this, where they gaue pro- [sig. Aiii[r]] lixe rules, I haue giuen briefe rules, where they gaue vncertaine rules, I haue giuen sure rules, and where they haue giuen no rules, I haue giuen rules. After all this that I haue said of their rules, I doe affirme that they deserued greater commendations aboue mee, for finding out the long way, then I aboue others for laying down the short way. For had not they opened the gappe, touching mee, it might very well hap that I should in no sort enter my selfe, and much lesse in any sort inuite others: nothing can at the beginning be perfected, and therefore are they to bee holden excused as the old verse hath:

> But ere the Painter can sure his craft attaine,
> Much froward facion transformeth hee in vayne,
> By raysing superfluitie, and adding that doth want,
> Rude Pictures are made both perfect and pleasant.
> For such things by negligence are left vndone,
> That by good diligence might be wonne.

There be sufficient, many, and firme prooues had of this that I say, which may by my rules be done, of which I will heere put downe some of them, though I get as little by being beleeued, as I should loose by being belyed.

In a moneth and lesse I instructed a child about the age of eight yeeres, to sing a good number of songs, difficult crabbed Songs, to sing at the first sight, to be so indifferent for all parts, alterations, Cleues, flats, and sharpes, that he could sing a part of that kinde, of which he neuer learned any song, which child for strangenesse was brought before the Lord Deputie of Ireland, to be heard sing: for there were none of his age, though he were longer at it, nor any of his time, (though he were elder) knowne beefore these [sig. Aiii[v]] rules to sing exactly.

There was another, that had before often handled Instruments, but neuer practised to sing (for hee could not name one Note) who hearing of these rules, obtayned in short time, such profit by them, that he could sing a difficult song of himselfe, without any Instructor.

There was another, who by dodging at it, hearkning to it, & harping vpon it, could neuer be brought to tune sharps aright, who so soone as hee heard these rules set downe for the same, could tune them sufficiently well. I haue taught diuerse others by these rules, in lesse then a moneth; what my selfe by the olde, obtained not in more then two yeeres. Diuerse other proofes I might

---

[c] Should read *and*.

recite, which heere as needlesse I doe omit, because the thing will shew it selfe. *Diuerse haue repented in their age that they were not put to sing in their youth; but seeing that by these rules, a good skill may be had in a moneth: and the wayes learned in foure or fiue dayes: none commeth too late to learne, and specially if this saying be true:* That no man is so olde but thinketh he may liue one yeere longer. *As Aristotle in setting forth his predicaments, saw many things requisite to be entreated off: and yet vnfit to be mixed with his treatise: he therefore made ante predicaments, and post predicaments: so I for the same cause (desirous to abolish confusion) haue added to my rules, ante rules, and post rules. Vale.*

[sig. Aiv^r]

The ante rules of Song.

To prepare for naming the Notes.

PRactise to sunder the Vowels and Consonants, distinctly pronouncing them according to the manner of the place.

To prepare for Quantitie.

PRactise to haue the breath long to continue, and the tongue at libertie to runne.

To prepare for Time.

PRactise in striking to keepe a iust proportion of one stroke to another.

To prepare for Tune.

PRactise to haue your voice cleere, which when thou hast done, learne the rules following.

The skill of song doth consist in foure things.
{
Naming.
Quantitie.
Time.
Tune.
}

[sig. Aiv^v]

Rules of Song.[3]

The Scale of Musick, which is called Gam-vt, conteineth 10 rules, and as many spaces; and is set downe in letters and sillables, in which you must beegin at the lowest word, Gam-vt, and so go vpwards to the end still ascending, and learne it perfectly without booke, to say it forwards and backewards: to know, wherein euery key standeth, whether in rule or in space: and how many Cliefes, how many Notes is contayned in euery Key.

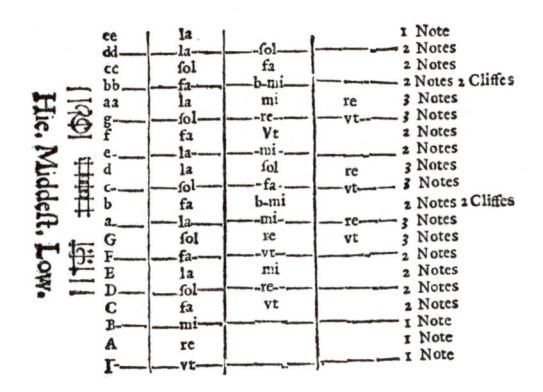

ee	la			1 Note
dd	la	fol		2 Notes
cc	fol	fa		2 Notes
bb	fa	b-mi		2 Notes 2 Cliffes
aa	la	mi	re	3 Notes
g	fol	re	vt	3 Notes
f	fa	Vt		2 Notes
e	la	mi		2 Notes
d	la	fol	re	3 Notes
c	fol	fa	vt	3 Notes
b	fa	b-mi		2 Notes 2 Cliffes
a	la	mi	re	3 Notes
G	fol	re	vt	3 Notes
F	fa	vt		2 Notes
E	la	mi		2 Notes
D	fol	re		2 Notes
C	fa	vt		2 Notes
B	mi			1 Note
A	re			1 Note
Γ	vt			1 Note

For Naming. Cap. primo.

There bee six names, Vt, Re, Mi, Fa, Sol, La. The order of ascention & descention with them is thus.

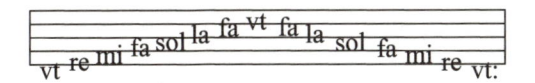

[sig. Avʳ]

Exceptions.

Change Vt, into Sol, change Re, into La, when the next removing Note is vnder.[4]

The Cleues whereby we know where the *Vt* standeth are thus marked as.

The *G*: cliefe is the mark of the higher *G sol re vt*. In the scale: & the *C*: clefe of that placed called *C sol fa vt*. And the *F*: cliefe of *F fa vt* the lower in the scale.

62   *A Briefe Introduction to the Skill of Song,* Part II

Now in this sort you may finde by the cliefe where euery note standeth: and least there should seeme any difficultie, I will begin from the first sight of the booke, that all things that doe belong to their knowledge, may bee the better vnderstoode. First when a man seeth the booke before him he may see certaine rules which goe along lineally by 5 and 5 which number of 5 is called a set of pricksong (for a set of plainesong hath commonly but 4. rules,) then he may see in the first of the set alwayes one of the foresayde cleifes vpon some rule, and whatsoeuer note standeth vpon the same rule with the cliefe, is said to be in that place wherof that cleife which [sig. Av^v] he seeth is the marke, and if any note stand in the next space aboue, it is said to stand in the next place aboue that place, whereof that cleife is the marke. And so vpward and downeward continually counting from the close as in this example.

The first note standeth in *C sol fa vt*, because it standeth vpon the same rule with the clief which is the mark of *C sol fa vt*, the second in *D la sol re*, because *D la sol re* is next aboue *C sol fa vt* in the scale of *Gam vt*: the third in *B fa b mi*, because it is in the next place beneah[d] *C sol fa vt*: the fourth in *E la mi*, because *E la mi* is the next place saue one to *C sol fa vt*, & the said fourth note standeth in the next place saue one to the cliefe which is the mark of the place *C sol fa vt*. And so of all other notes: then in the ende of the set, hee may see a thing thus

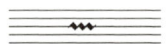

marked, which is called a direct, because it is alwayes put vpon the rule or space wherein the first of the next set standeth, and doth so direct a man, euen as in bookes the word that is lowest vpon euery side of the leafe doth direct a man to the word next following.

The rule of Vt.

The next thing necessary to be knowne for the right naming of notes, is the place where that note standeth which is named *Vt*. And as by counting vpward and downeward from the cliefe it is to bee knowne where euery note standeth, so it is to be knowne by counting vpward and downeward from that which is called *Vt*, what the right name of euery note is: but first let vs set downe how the place where the *vt* standeth is knowen, [sig. Avi^r] which is thus. There be three places, in one of which the *vt* must alwaies be: that is to say, in *G*, which is

---

[d] Should read *beneath*.

Gamvt and *G sol re vt*, when there is no flat in *C*, which is *C fa vt*, *C sol fa vt*, and *C sol fa*, when there is a flat in *b mi*, or *b fa b mi*. In *F* which is *F fa vt*, when there are two flats, one in *b mi* or *b fa b mi*, the other in *E la mi*, or *E la*.[5]

As for example.

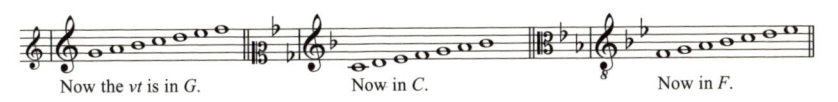

[musical notation: Now the *vt* is in G.   Now in C.   Now in F.]

¶No b flat, the *(vt)* in G. The b flat in b onely, the *(vt)* in C. The b flat in b and E, the *(vt)* in F.

1 G putteth Vt to the same place.[6]
2 ⎫
3 ⎬ F. and B. to the next vp, as.
   ⎭

[musical notation: 1   2   3]

4 C putteth *Vt* to the fift place vp, and from C down to the fourth. B, taketh place of the rest.
   B, is placed last to shew that it taketh place of the rest.
5 If there commeth two, b.b. being a fourth, the vpper taketh place.
6 And being a fift, the nether taketh place, as:

[musical notation: 4   5   6]

[musical notation: 7   8]

[sig. Avi^v]
7 D. putteth *Vt* to the fift place downe, but it is seldome vsed.
8 If there commeth two b.b. being a second a sunder, the vpper[e] taketh place, which chanceth very rare.[7]

More shall be sayd of naming in the chapter of tuning.

When you haue in this sort found out the *vt*, you must vnderstand that euery note that standeth in the next place aboue it is named *re*, euery note that standeth in the next place to that is named *mi*, in the next to that *fa*, then *sol*, then *la*, then *fa*, ascending vp alwaies orderly, counting the rules, and spaces:

[e] Should read *lower*; see below, n. 7.

then next aboue that againe is *vt*: for you shall finde that place, which is the eight place from that wherein your other *vt* stood, to begin with the same letter: So that if the rules & spaces were infinite, you might in this manner giue euery note his right name: and as you did count vpward *Vt, re, mi, fa, sol, la, fa*, and so come againe to *vt*: so must you come downeward from *vt*, the same way backward, by *fa, la, sol, fa, mi, re, vt*. And so come to *fa*, againe. And in this sort the right name of euery note is knowne. Two things from these rules are excepted, the one is, that euery *re*, should be named *la*, when you ascend to it, or descend from it: and that euery *vt*, should bee named *sol*, which two things are vsed *euphoniæ gratia*, and yet this name of *vt*, is most proper to the base or lowest part in the first place.[8]

Obiection against the latter exception.

In the latter exception it is said, that *vt* should be alwaies changed into *sol*, therefore seeing it is neuer vsed, [sig. Avii^r] it is in vaine placed in all this former tractation.[9]

Solution. It is placed in all this former tractation for two causes, the one is, that it should be distinguished by the name from the other *sol*, and the other is, because it hath bene a name vsed from the beginning, and now commonly changed into *sol, euphoniæ gratia*: it may sometimes neuerthelesse be vsed, for (as I sayd before) the cunning singing man keeping euery note in his right tune, may name it according to his pleasure, for these names be no necessary accidents, for you see daylie that when any song is lettred, these names be not attributed to them, though then they be sung in their owne order, according to the opinion of many, yea very many.[10] I know I should adde a third exception, that is to say, to except also, that euery note hauing a sharpe beefore it, should be named *mi*, as in this example,

the third note.[11] And because that of that opinion there bee so many, I will for them shew a probable reason as by our principles may be shewed: then after by resoluing them, shewe what is most profitable, not refuting the opinion as an errour, beecause that looking to the matter, wee may finde that they may bee named as well *mi*, as *fa*, insomuch as the names (as I sayd before) are no necessary accidents, but neuerthelesse, because heere we seeke the most apt name, it were vnfit to passe it ouer.[12] Wherefore the principall argument for them wee may in this sort forme.

Obiection. We should name all notes so neare as wee can, according as such notes are named in the *gamvt*, for it is certain, that these are the names which are most fit, [sig. Avii^v] for so in the beginning by the first inuentors of

Musick they haue bene set downe: but no note that is sharp in the *gamvt* is named *fa*, therefore no note made sharp by a collaterall reason, should bee named *fa*. Secondly, throughout all the *gam vt*, from *sol* to *fa*. Next vnder it is a whole note, but from that *sol* to that *fa*, if we should call it *fa*, is but halfe a note, therefore if we call it *fa*, wee breake altogether the rule of *gamvt*, which wee should obserue: thirdly euery place in the *gam vt* that is sharp, is named either *mi* or *la*.[13] Therefore this note (beecause not so aptly *la*) must be named *mi*. Before we fully satisfie these arguments, one thing must necessarily be knowen: that is to say, that in naming the notes in *gam vt* the first inuentors did obserue two things, whereof the one was, to name the notes according to the *vt*: the other, to name euery note which is sharpe (as the argument proueth) *mi*, or *la*: and it falleth out sometimes, when notes flat by collaterall reasons are made sharp, that one of these two must necessarily be violated, that is to say, that eyther the note must not bee named according to the *vt*, or a note sharp must bee named *fa*, so that the controuersie lyeth in knowing, whether of these two should soonest be obserued: so according to this we answere to their arguments.[14] To the first, where they impute a fault in vs for naming a note sharp, *fa*, seeing that no sharp note in all the *gam vt* is named *fa*, we may impute an other absurditie to them, seeing they would haue the next note vnder *sol*, *mi*, which is not found in all *gam vt*, which is the more absurditie (as we will proue in the solution to the third argument) To the second, the solu- [sig. Aviii^r] tion is easie, that euen as euery *sol* to *fa*, next vnder it is a whole note: so from euery *sol* to *mi*, next vnder it is more: so that according to the *gam vt*, in that respect none of them is true. To the third wee answere, that it may bee as well *la*, as *mi*, because that if ther were any reason why it should not be as well *la*, it might well be, to eschew this absurditie, that then in two places together there should bee one name, because the next vnder it is also *la*, but by naming it *mi*, the same absurditie commeth in another place, therefore the one is as absurd as the other, as in this example, where two

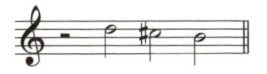

places together must according to them bee named *mi*, but to name two places together with one name, there is none but will think more dissonant, then to name them with diuers, whatsoeuer: for if a man did name *mi*, six times together in one place, beeing quauers, the one comming fast vpon the other, would make them seeme as though it were *mim, mim, mim*, as for example, whereby it plainely appeareth that this is most absurd. But because that it were as good that our selues should bring that, which others may do, by sharp grating vpon our solutions, in this sort we may frame a reply.[15] Let vs suppose, that in the middle of a song which had *fa* in *C sol fa vt*, there came two notes, one in *C sol fa vt*, & another in *B fa b mi*, hauing a flat before it, then if the latter note in *B fa b mi*, hauing the flat before it, be not called *fa*, it is against the order of the *vt*, which by the solutions should most be kept, if it be named *fa*, then commeth the absurditie proued in the [sig. Aviii^v] last example: that is, that two places together should haue one name, and likewise if six quauers did come in that sort, the fast comming of the one vpon the other, would make them seeme to be *faf, faf, faf*, which is as absurd and dissonant, as *mim, mim, mim*.

Resolution. Of the flat so comming, and of the sharp, there is not like reason, because that the flat so comming should alter the *vt*, so that as many notes as had come in *C sol fa vt*, after the flat, should be named *sol*, and not *fa*, but for the first note, & the second, they must be both *fa*, neuerthelesse because there may not be many of them together, as there may be of *mi*, & because that in quauers, twise *fa*, in that sort likely neuer chanceth, the one is not so absurd as the other.

Replication. It is graunted by the last solution, that the flat so comming should alter the *vt*, but to alter the *vt*, doth alter the key (which is in musick a great absurditie) therefore by the last solution, there is a great absurditie graunted.

Solution. It is graunted conditionally, that is to say, if the like happened (as in the argument obiected) though sometimes in the middest of a song, to change the key, and come into it againe, is allowed. Wherefore for the names, being the least necessary and most troublesome accident, let this suffice.

For Quantitie. Cap. 2.[16]

There be eight quantities whereof euery one hath his proper marke, and proper rest, as followeth.

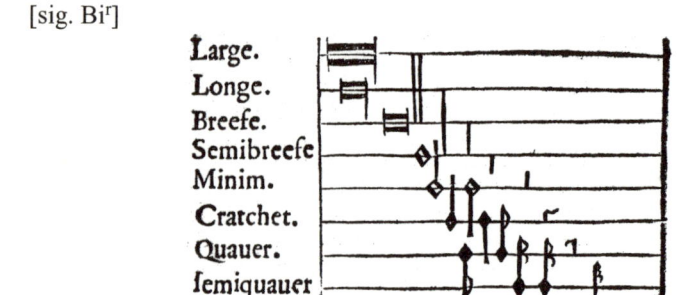

[sig. Bi^r]

Large.
Longe.
Breefe.
Semibreefe
Minim.
Cratchet.
Quauer.
ſemiquauer

The proportion that these quantities hath one to another is that there should goe two of euery one to the next vpward as two semiquauers, to a quauer, two quauers to a cratchet, two cratchets to a minim, &c.

To these are reduced the quantities of proportions, as where there goeth three cratchets to a minim length of which the black semibreefe comprehendeth two, & ther the minim rest is but as long as one of these cratchets.

Heere note that the prick is in quantitie half so long as the note before it: as a prick after a large, is in quantitie as a long &c.

Prickes of diuision are vsed to separate diuersitie of kindes in quantitie.

For Time. Cap. 3.

There be 2. kindes of time, Semibreefe time, & three [sig. Bi^v] minim time. Semibrefe time is the striking vp & downe of the hand equally in length continuing. Three minim time is the striking downe & the vp of the hand equally in length, making each latter stroke, iust halfe of the former. The marke of the former kinde of time is.

The marke of the latter is.

In tuning Songs of Semibreefe time, you must put of the notes, as much as maketh a minim length to euery mouing of the hand, likewise in the minim time, saue that to euery stroke there goeth but a minim length.

Heere note that these two kindes of time, may be deuided into minim time, by keeping all strokes equall in length, putting a minim length to euery whole stroke.

For Tune. Cap. 4.

There be eight notes, whose ascention, and descention doe comprehend all tunes, as the roote doth the tree, be they neuer so difficult, with flats and Sharps, who so knew how to vse them, the notes are common, the vse is rare, or not yet found, which being knowen, will giue great light to Musitions, & breed great ease to Singing men, the eight notes are these that follow, as:

The tune of these eight Notes is to be learned by practise, and to be beleeued as a principle in Musicke.

Tune the first Note of any song as it serueth best for the voyce.

[sig. Bii[r]]

If the Note from which and to which you goe, be both according to the Vt, of the Song, count according to the eight notes altogether.[17]

If the note to which you goe bee altered by some intermingled flat, then for comptings sake name the Note from which you goe, as well as the note to which you goe, according to the *Vt*, of that intermingled flat, and in so doing take great care not to loose the tune of the note from which you compt, as,[18]

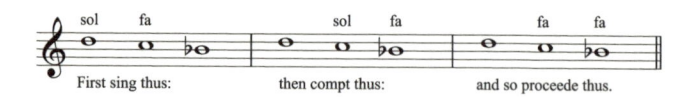

If the Note to which you goe, be altered in tune by some intermingled sharp, obserue both in the note from which and to which you goe, this Rule.

Compt to the tune of sharps by the Vt, put down to the third place, when you haue thus compting by wrong names gotten the right tunes, giue the right names after, as:[19]

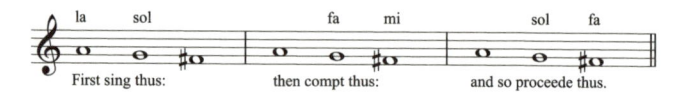

The sharp may be put in the vpper fa, in the nether fa, and in Vt.[20]

The sharp in the Vt, taketh place of the sharp in the vpper or nether fa, for by the Vt of it, the other two places should be sharp, the rest of the places remaining na- [sig. Bii[v]] turally: as,[21]

Vt for compting.

Likewise the sharp in the nether fa, taketh place of the sharp in the vpper fa, for by the Vt of the ♯ in the nether fa, the vpper fa must bee sharp, the rest remaining naturally: as,[22]

Vt for Compting.

The flat may be put in two places, in Mi, and in La, also it is common in Mi, but not so common in La: also if the flat be in La (according to the Vt of it) Mi must be flat: as,[23]

Heere note that for to tune sharps, put downe Vt, to the third place.

If the note to which you goe may neither in tuning nor naming belong to one order of ascention, go back to the note before, and so Compt: as,[24]

First begin thus, Then go back thus, and so proceed thus.

[sig. Biii^r]

As men name according to the *Vt*, of the flat, so there be, that (for facility & fitnesse of the name to the tune) do name according to the *Vt* of the sharp sometimes: as,[25]

Heere note, that the intermingled flat beareth force but whilest notes as appendant come in the same place, though for handsomnesse men name beefore or after according to it: Likewise the sharp, as,[26]

Thappendancy of the flat by the sharp, and of the sharp by the Flat is taken away, though by negligence and ignorance of prickers, we are oft driuen to gather thappendancie by the course of the song. Looke in the last example.[27]

The prick is to be continued and kept in one tune with the note before it.

Heere note, that the Cleues may remoue from one rule to another, and that they are vsed for Flats.[28] Also that the Direct is put to shew the note following: as,

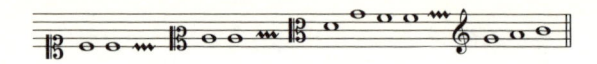

70   *A Briefe Introduction to the Skill of Song*, Part II

Euery Note in the order of Ascension is a whole [sig. Biii^v] note or tone aboue the next vnder, saue the vpper & nether Fa, which be but halfe notes or Semitones.

For readinesse in setting Notes distant, let the learner practise these examples following, with all such things as make varietie in naming, or tuning.

Also for readines, note that euery foure rules & a space further, maketh an eight, & euery eight, hath like names.[29]

vt mi re fa mi sol fa la la fa sol mi fa re mi vt re vt

sol fa la sol mi la fa fa sol sol fa fa la mi sol re fa sol

sol la sol fa sol sol la sol mi sol fa sol sol la sol fa sol sol sol.

sol la fa sol la la mi fa fa fa sol la fa sol la fa sol sol fa mi fa fa la sol sol la sol

Edition   71

[sig. Biv^r]

Fa sol fa la fa sol fa la la mi fa sol fa sol la fa fa fa la sol fa.

[In the original, the voices are printed as separate parts, in the order soprano, tenor, alto, bass, and sharps rather than natural signs are used to cancel flats.][30]

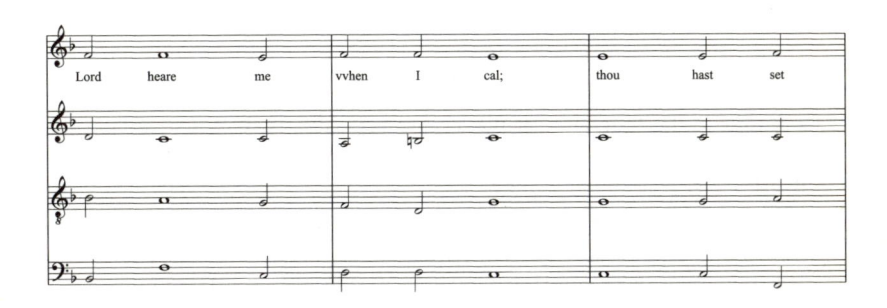

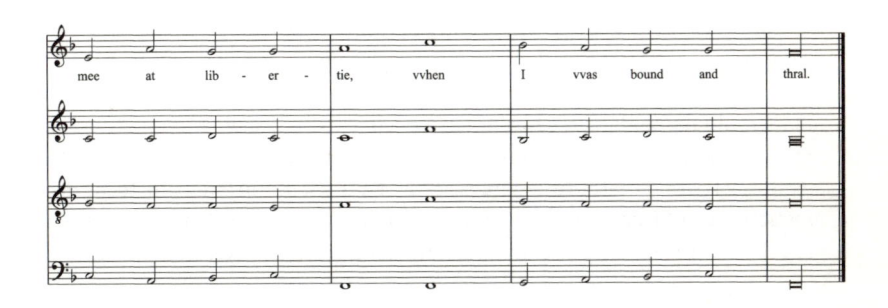

O God   that art my   right - eous - nesse,

The Church Tune.

Lord heare me vvhen I cal; thou hast set

mee at lib - er - tie, vvhen I vvas bound and thral.

[Musical notation with syllables:]

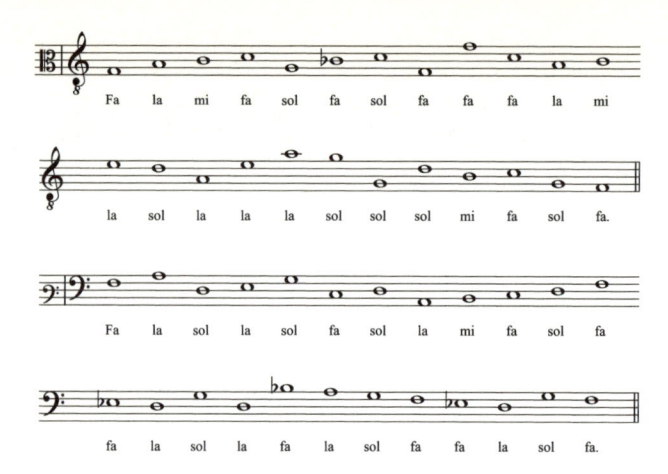

Fa la mi fa sol fa sol fa fa fa la mi

la sol la la la sol sol sol mi fa sol fa.

Fa la sol la sol fa sol la mi fa sol fa

fa la sol la fa la sol fa fa la sol fa.

[sig. Biv^v]

The post rules of Song.

Heere followeth the post rules of Song, which are reduced to the vnlimited obseruations vsed in Singing.

For naming. Cap. I.

THe exceptions from the order of ascention & descention are diuersely vsed according to the diuersitie of place, and accordingly, they are to bee giuen, for each order in naming seemeth best to them that haue beene brought vp withall.

D, is sometimes vsed in old songs as a Cleue, and putteth Vt downe to the fift place.

In Italy (as I vnderstand) they change Vt into Sol: in England they change Re, into La: when the next remouing Note before or after be vnder.

Some there bee that vse sometimes in defending at this day, the names of Re, and Vt, there be that name at randon,[f] some for pleasure, and some through ignorant imagination, often times beareth great force in making a thing seeme comely, or vncomely, as if in comming downe, Sol, Fa, La, Sol, a man should name the first two notes Re Mi, it would seeme to a singing man very vncomely: yet if the singing man did imagin, that the singer were putting a dittie, or word of foure sillables, [sig. Bv^r] as: Remigrare, to these foure Notes, he would not think it vncomely, & yet in doing the deed; both waies are all one, for the first two sillables of, Remigrare, are Re, Mi.[31]

---

[f] Should read *random*.

For Quantitie. Cap. II.[32]

TO make one and the selfe same mark of quantitie sometimes long, and sometimes short, Musitions in old time, borrowed colours of the Painters, sometimes making it red, and sometimes black, &c.

They borrowed numbers of Arithmatike, somtimes making this, and sometimes that figure, &c.

They borrowed Circles and Semicircles of Geometrie, sometimes putting in the Center or a lyne, & sometimes leauing it out, &c. Sometimes also thereby signifying alteration in time.

They borrowed similitudes of Philosophie, sometimes leauing fulnesse, and sometimes Eclips, as appeareth in the Moone, sometimes knitting and sometimes loosing, as in generation and corruption.

They vsed moreouer many signes and tokens and marks of Quantitie, that are cut off as superfluous.

They vsed also manifold names to distinguish these things one from another, to the wonderfull pestering of the memory, & great toile of the vnderstanding, though some of them wer necessary, yet many were superflous.

The Quantities in Proportion are diuers, according to the diuersitie of Proportions, which are *infinite in potentia*, that is to say, in possibilitie of increase, as number is.

Many of these things are yet vsed, as the Semibreefe [sig. Bv^v] rest, in three minim time, for three minim rests.

Some strange markes and knitting of Notes which time I doubt not will cut off, neuerthelesse heere shall follow examples of some, to which the redsidue[g] are to be reduced.

---

[g] Should read *residue*.

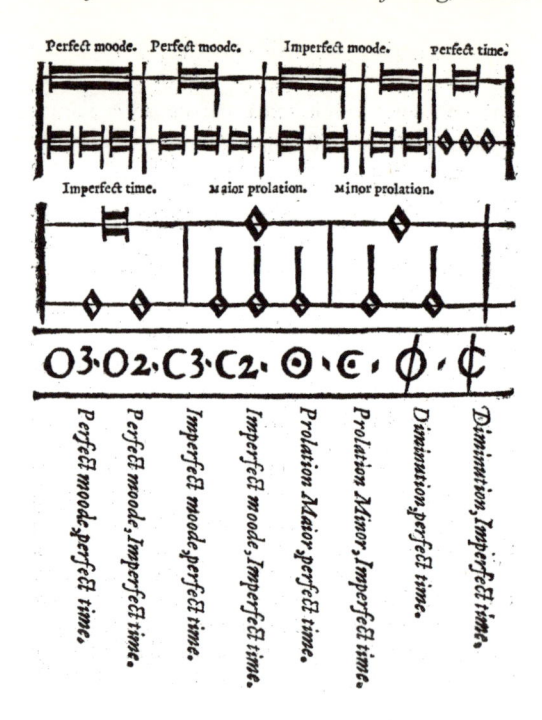

[sig. Bvi^r]

By these examples following, the foure Modes are knowne what qua*n*titie the lesser notes are to the greater.

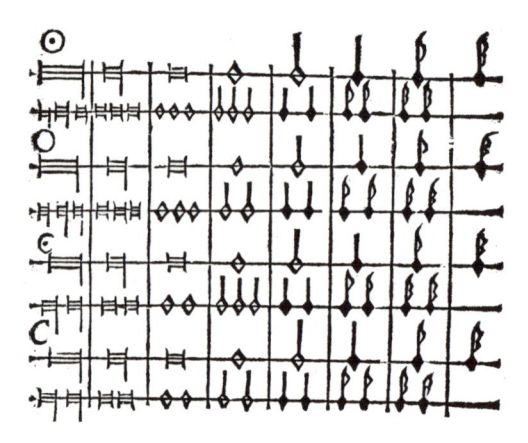

The lovver notes are as much in quantitie as the higher vvith their pricks.

Pricks of Diuision are those, vvhich are set aboue notes and not by them, and they shevv the note to bee perfect before the prick: and the note follovving doth belong to another stroke.

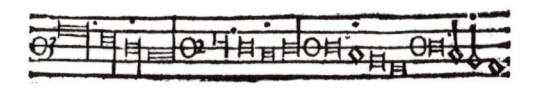

[sig. Bvi^v]

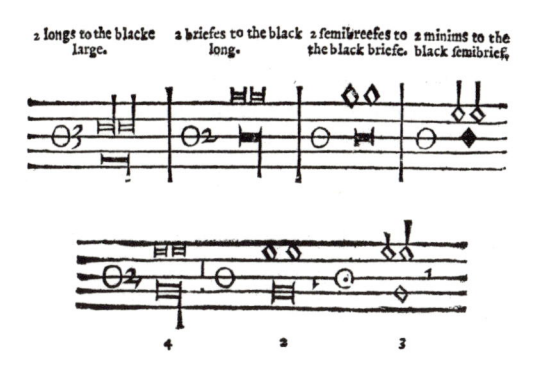

XII Examples of Legatures.

More Examples of Legatures, as followeth.

[sig. Bvii^r]

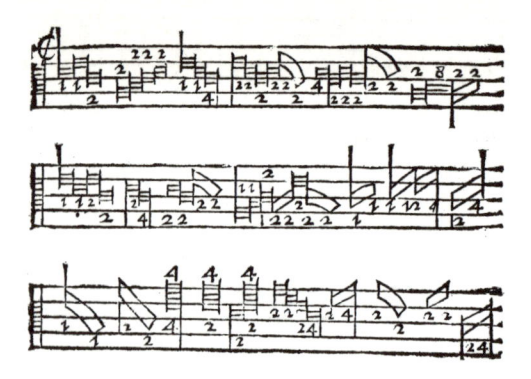

For Time. Cap.III.

IN timing hard proportions that go odding, many take care onely of the whole stroke, wholy kept without deuiding it to the going vp & then downe agayne of the hand.

Some keepe Semibreefe time, as sufficient easie of it selfe, and doe not diuide it into minim time.

Three minim time is more difficult, and therefore some doe diuide it into minim time: as,

Take a stick of a certaine length, and a stone of a certaine weight, hold the stick standing vpon an end of [sig. Bvii^v] some table: See you haue vpon the stick diuers marks: hold the stone vp by the side of the stick: then as you let fall the stone, instantly begin to sing one Note, and iust with the noyse that it maketh vpon the table, beegin another Note, and as long as thou holdest the first Note, so long hold the rest, and let that note thy Cratchet or thy Minim, &c. as thou seest cause, and thus maist thou measure the very Time it selfe that thou keepest, and know whether thou hast altered it, or not.

For Tune. Cap.IIII.

SOme learne to Tune only by the Voice of anoher:[h] some vse helpe of an Instrument, which is the better way.

---

[h] Should read *another*.

Learners vse to tune by a certaine continuance of time, according to the *Vt* of the song, before they practise intermingled Flats or sharps.

Heere note, that C. called Csolfavt cleue, is a fift beneth G. called Gsolrevt cleue, and F. called Ffavt cleue, is a fift beneth C. called Csolfavt, Cleue.

Also a man may compt from any cleue, by the letters, compting them forward when hee goeth vpward, and acompting them backward when he goeth downward, telling but the first seuen letters: by the knowledge of this, men may giue their tunes to the parts without knowledge of the Gamvt. Yet for the common vse, it were not amisse, that learners should sometime or other commit the Gam-vt to memory.

Many things are heere taught by rule, for which [sig. Bviii[r]] teachers heeretofore, gaue no rule, and if they were asked how shall a man know the like? they would answere, that is according to the course of the Song, but this answere is so vncertaine, that it is as good for the yong Scoller, they had said we know not.

¶A generall Table comprehending two parts in one, of all kindes vpon all plaine Songs, vpon all pricke Songs, and in all wayes that may be found, one part beginning, th'other following, the plaine Song or ground being sung beneth them: all which are found by this present table, which such facilitie, that the vpper part is made, and neuer booked, as heere followeth.

[sig. Bviii^v]

The obseruations of the places vp are sixe	6 5 4 3 2 1	8 1 7 2 5 1	11 7 6 1 6 2	10 6 5 7 7 3	9 5 4 6 1 4	8 4 3 5 2 5	7 3 2 4 3 6	6 2 1 3 4 7
Places vp.	1	7	6	5	4	3	2
Courses vp. 1 / Courses dovvne.	1356	6	135	16	35	136	5
2	7 6	135	16	35	136	5	1356
3	6 135	16	35	136	5	1356	6
4	5 16	35	136	5	1356	6	135
5	4 35	136	5	1356	6	135	36
6	3 136	5	1356	6	135	16	35
7	2 5	1356	6	135	16	35	136
8 vt su: 1	1356	6	135	16	35	136	5
Places dovvn	1	2	3	4	5	6	7
The obseruations of the places down are sixe.	1 1 2 5 3 2 4 7 5 1 6 5	2 2 6 2 3 1 2 6	3 3 7 4 2 3 7	4 4 1 5 2 3 4 8	5 5 2 6 4 5 9	6 6 3 7 5 6 10	7 7 4 1 6 7 11

[sig. Ci^r]

THis present table, may serue also, who so marketh it well, for 2 parts in one, without a plaine song, of all kinds, & in all waies for 3 parts in one, without a plainsong, or ground, the third part being vnder: of all kindes & of all wayes for 2 parts in one, vpon 2 plain songs, or grounds at once, for maintaining reports, & other such things as these be.

 First it is to be vnderstanded by this word place, is ment the distance of the following part, to the former part, as the same place or vnison, is called the first place, the next or second place is called the second place, whether it be vp or downe, &c.[33]

 Next heere is to be vnderstanded that by this word, Course, is ment the distaunce of that which followeth iust so long after, as the following part resteth to that which goeth beefore, in the plaine Song or ground, as if the following part haue a Semibreefe rest, then the Note of tbe[i] ground is in the first course, which hath in the same place that which followeth, iust a

---

[i] Should read *the*.

Semibreefe length after, and that note is in the second course, which hath in the second place that which followeth iust a Semibreefe length after, whether it bee vp or downe, &c.³⁴

This beeing knowne, first looke in what place vp or downe, you would haue the following part to bee, which is according to the pleasure of the maker, and so it is how long the following part shall rest. Then looke in what course vp or downe is the note of the ground, for which you would make, then looke what square of the table meeteth with the place and course, and there [sig. Ciᵛ] you shall finde noted by figures, what concord serueth for that course.³⁵

All Concords nextʲ expressed in the square, make discords betwixt the vpper part and the plaine song or ground. Neuerthelesse, they may be brought in, when they may be garded by the place next adioyning, for whatsoeuer maketh a discord, the next place to it maketh a concord.

Note also that iust so long before the close, as the following part resteth, you make not that which breedeth a discord, betwixt the vpper part and the ground, nor that which to the close of the ground is one more in number then the second figure of obseruation.

Note also, that if iust so long before the close as the following part resteth, you make that which to the close is two more in number then the first figure of obseruation, then the best way is to make it sharp.

Note also, that from the beginning forth, of so farre before the close, as the following part resteth, all concords serueth.

*The exposition of the figure of obseruation.*³⁶

THe first and second figures sheweth what distances (in respect of the latter notes of the course) should not come twise together, remouing one way with the latter notes, and also where in respect of the latter note of the course, a [sig. Ciiʳ] flat for a sharp, or a sharp for a flat, contrary to the order of the place should not bee.

The third & fourth sheweth what mouing one way with the place, iust so long after as the following part resteth, maketh discords.

The fift and sixt serueth wherein the distance, there should not be like mouing one way with the place iust so long after as the following part resteth, and the fift figure. Also where sharp for flat, or flat for sharp, contrary to the order of the place should not bee iust so long after as the following resteth.

Heere note, that vnder each number are comprehended all those that maketh eights, or concords, of that kinde to it, except that vnder the last figure of obseruation such as make eights to the number one way with the place, and such as make ninthes to it in the contrary way are comprehended.

ʲ Should read *not*; see above, p. 53, n. 102.

Heere note that two parts in one in the vnizon, fourth, and fift, doe differ from the rest, for in the rest, both parts are tyed, to like order of ascention, but in these both parts do keepe like order according to their place.

Note also, that in two parts in one, in the fourth vp, and in the fift downe, the vpper fa, kept flat in the nether parts causeth a strange flat to be brought in the vpper part, therefore the best way is to make it sharp, vnlesse it bee in such places as a strange flat will doe well to come in.

[sig. Cii^v]

Two verses comprehending the foresaid Table, which for necessities sake of the matter, must be vvritten crossing one another[37]

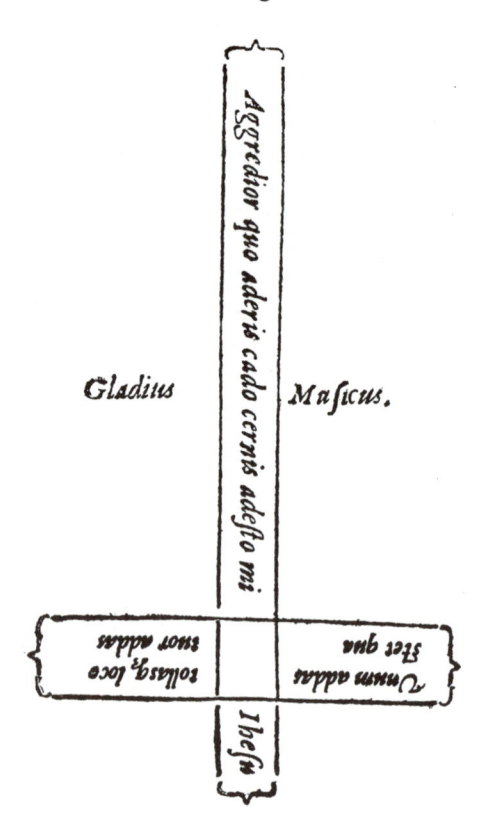

Gladius | *Musicus.*

[sig. Ciii^r]
IN this Table or figure aforesayde, foure things are comprehended,[38] the places, the 6. figures of obseruation belonging to them, the courses and concords seruing for them, for the seuen places, there be seuen words in the blade of the Sword: the first word, *Aggredior*, is alwaies for the first place: the

second word downward, *quo*, is for the second place downeward, &c. And the second word vpward, *mi*, is for the second place vpward, &c. This word, I*hesu*, is cut off from the rest, to signifie that it beelongeth to another kinde, for in it the letters numerable being 5. doe signifie the first and second figures of obseruation, and it is written one way with the verse, to signifie that it goeth according to the woord of the verse, which is for the place, for it signifieth one number with the word of the verse, that standeth for the place, as if the word bee the fourth word of the verse, then it signifieth, 4. &c. and 5. signifieth the fift number, to that, as the fift number to foure is 8. and so are the first and second figures of obseruation found. Then are the other foure figures of obseruation to bee found by the crosse verse, which sayth: adde one to the place, take one from the place, let the place stand, adde foure to the place, and so shall you finde the third, fourth, fift, and sixt figures of obseruation.

Heere note, that if the place be the vnizon, beecause you cannot take one from a vnizon, take it from eight, which is of the same kinde, when you haue thus done, tourne the poynt of the Sword downe, and then the seuen woords, serueth for the seuen courses in this order: First the word that serueth for the place, serueth for the [sig. Ciii^v] first course, the second woord vpward, for the second course vpward: the second woord downeward, for the second course downward, &c. As the Sword now standeth, compting about vpon the seuen words, when you haue found what woord serueth for the course, looke what vowels bee in it, and thereby you shall know the concords, that serueth for that course, as if the vowell bee A, it signifieth the vnizon. If it be E, it signifieth the third. If it bee I, it signifieth the fift. And if it be O, it signifieth the sixt. Lo, thus are all the things expressed at large in the table, briefely contriued in the compasse of two verses.

[sig. Civ^r]
The names of the Cords for Counterpoint, Descant, and any set Song in how many parts soeuer.

A concord is diuided into an { Vnizon. Third..^{k} Fift. Sixt. Eight. Tenth. Twelfth. Thirtenth. & a Fiftenth } Discord are these. { A second. A fourth. A seuenth. A Ninth. A leuenth A fouretenth. } & their eights.

---

^{k} Two points in original.

82   *A Briefe Introduction to the Skill of Song*, Part II

Concords, perfect and vnperfect:

[sig. Civ^v]

Discords.

Concords.

[sig. Cv^r]

De Inuentione.[39]

CRescit in infinitum, Inuentio tempore cuncto,
  Sed tribus est dixis sæpe morata malis.

Est mora paupertas prohibens Inuenta probari,
  Non poterit fieri stultus inanis ait.

Vis, piger inquit, adire via latitante leone?
  Sic mora pauperies, stultus, homoq; piger.

Laus nunc, laus semper, laus omni tempore summo:
Discens atq; docens, dicite: lausq; Deo.

FINIS.

[sig. Cv^v–Cvi^r]
[In the original, the psalm is printed in choirbook format, and sharps rather than natural signs are used to cancel flats.][40]

84   *A Briefe Introduction to the Skill of Song*, Part II

Be-hold hovv I doe still la-ment, my sinnes vvher-ein I doe off-end: O Lord for them shall I bee-shent, sith thee to please I doe en-tend.

[sig. Cvi^v]
   10. sundry waies of 2. parts in one vpon the plain song.[41]

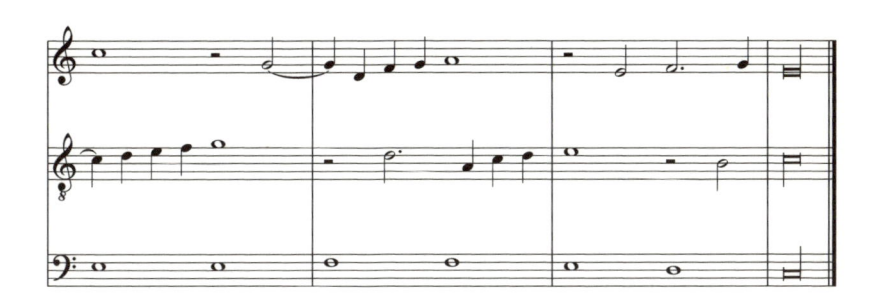

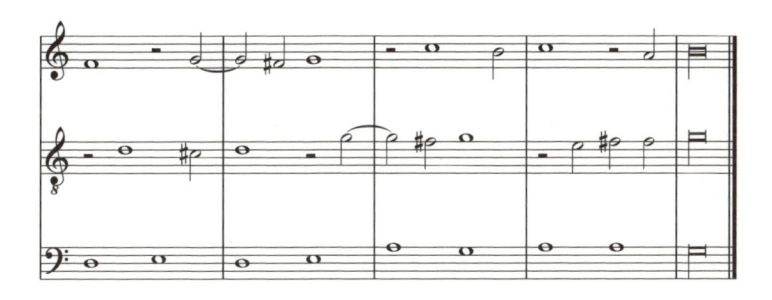

A Briefe Introduction to the Skill of Song, Part II

[sig. Cvii^r]

Edition

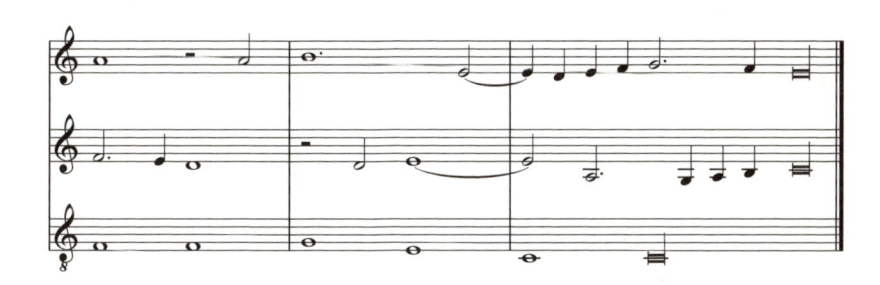

[sig. Cvii^v]

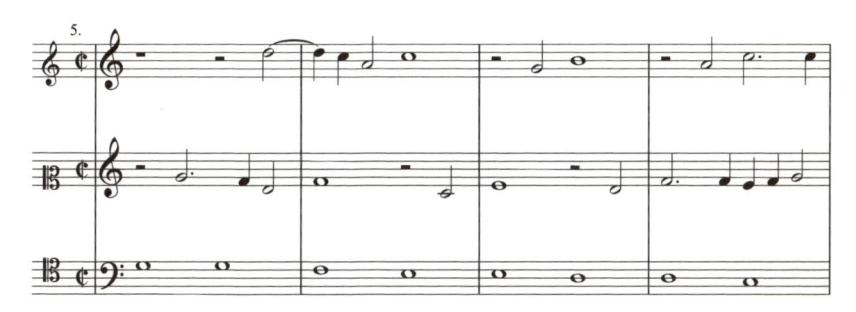

[sig. Cviiiʳ]

Edition

[sig. Cviiiᵛ]

FINIS. Place the Table of the comparisons of Cliffes after this.

Edition 91

[foldout page]
A Table of the comparisons of Cliffe, how one followeth another for the naming of Notes: changing (Vt) *into* (Sol) *and* (Re) *into* (La.)

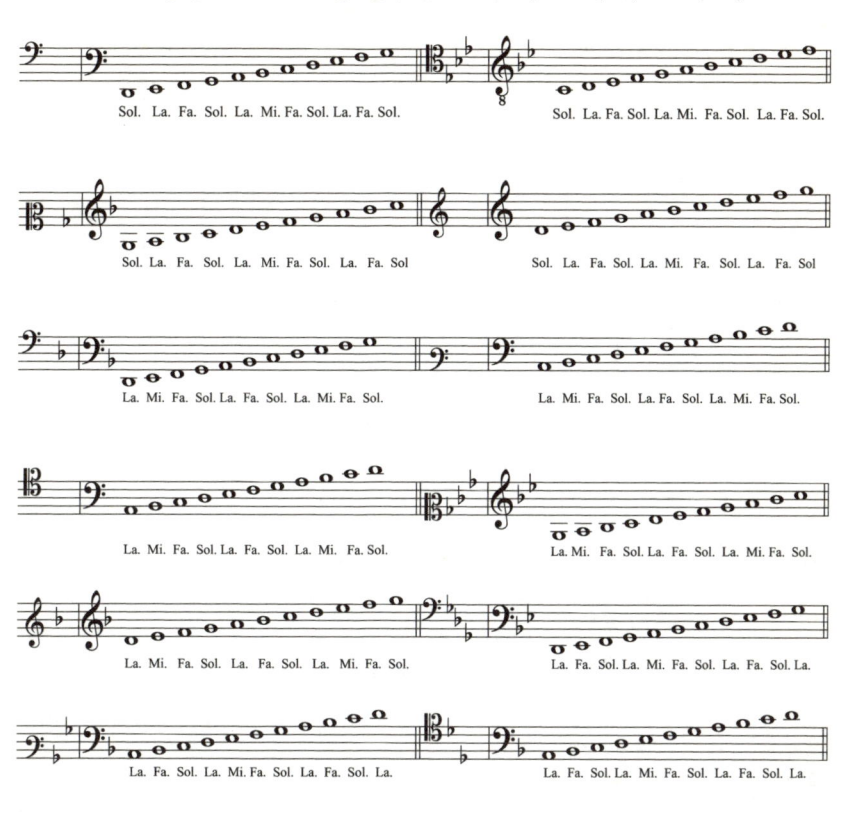

A Briefe Introduction to the Skill of Song, Part II

Notes

[1] 'Music is a respectable and agreeable pleasure especially suitable to free men.'

[2] 'And I have given my heart to know prudence, and learning, and errors, and folly: and I have perceived that in these also there was labour, and vexation of spirit' (Eccles. 1: 17).

[3] 'Rules of Song' appears as a running header on sigs. Aiv^v–Cii^r and Ciii^r–Cv^r It is possible that this label was intended as a section heading comparable to 'The ante rules of Song' (sig. Aiv^r) and 'The post rules of Song' (sig. Biv^v), and that the printer inadvertently set it as a running head.

[4] The syllables *ut* and *re* should be used only when they refer to the lowest notes in a passage. When they are not (that is, 'when the next removing Note is vnder' one or the other of the notes to which these syllables refer), the notes should be renamed *sol* and *la*.

[5] Bathe's point here, that the location of *ut* is determined by the presence or absence of signature flats, is partly obscured by the inconsistent punctuation used in this passage. The three places in which *ut* may be found are (1) on G, when there are no signature flats; (2) on C, when there is a signature flat on B; and (3) on F, when there are signature flats on B and E.

[6] In this part of Bathe's text, the author restates the 'Rule of Vt' so as to enable his readers to find the location of *ut* by considering only the clef or combination of clefs that appear at the beginning of a passage of music. See the discussion in Part I, pp. 22–27.

[7] Although Bathe's text reads 'the vpper taketh place', this appears to be an error. All three of the 'orders of ascention' discussed so far in the treatise (with no flats and *ut* on G; with one flat and *ut* on C; and with two flats and *ut* on F) are characterized by the interval of a minor seventh between *ut* and the seventh degree above *ut* (*fa*). The three-flat system to which Bathe refers here will be intervallically identical to the no-flat, one-flat and two-flat systems previously described only if *ut* is located on B♭. In order for the student to identify this *ut* correctly, he would need to recognize that the lower flat 'taketh place' for the purpose of finding its location. Having determined that the A flat 'taketh place', the student would recall that *ut* lies one whole tone above the pitch thus marked – in other words, on B♭ (compare Bathe's directives nos. 5 and 6, above). The 'order of ascention' associated with this system is as follows: *ut* (B♭), *re* (C), *mi* (D), *fa* (E♭), *sol* (F), *la* (G), *fa* (A♭), *ut* (B♭).

[8] The two exceptions that Bathe raises to the normal rules governing the naming of pitches are the same as those stated previously on sig. Av^r: 'Change Vt, into Sol, change Re, into La, when the next removing Note is vnder.' In order to defend the validity of these exceptions, Bathe will rely on the rhetorical strategy of *objection and answer* (on the general characteristics of this strategy, see above, pp. 18–21). Having begun the discussion of this issue by advancing his argument (that *ut* and *re* should be renamed *sol* and *la* when they do not refer to the lowest notes in a passage), he will proceed to provide a hypothetical *objection* to this argument. Then he will offer a *solution* (an *answer*) to this objection by refuting the arguments offered in support of it, and thereby confirming for his readers the validity of his own original assertion.

[9] As a rhetorical *objection* to his first two exceptions, Bathe argues that, if one were to rename as *sol* every pitch originally named *ut*, then the syllable *ut* would lose its meaningful place within the solmization system described thus far.

[10] Bathe resolves the hypothetical dispute about renaming *ut* and *re* as *sol* and *la* by claiming that (1) the syllable *ut* is useful in some contexts in that it enables one to

distinguish by name between the first and fifth degrees of the standard 'order of ascension'; and (2) the names *ut* and *re* should be retained within his solmization system out of a respect for tradition. In the end, however, the well-trained singer (the 'cunning singing man') may name the notes of a passage however he or she wishes so long as proper tuning is maintained.

11 As a third exception to his basic solmization rules, Bathe suggests that every note preceded by an accidental sharp should be named *mi*. Unlike his first two exceptions, however, the third proves to be a rhetorical 'straw man' that he will attempt to discredit in order to defend his own, contravening view – that accidental sharps do not affect the solmization of a passage. Following the principles of the rhetorical strategy of *objection and answer*, Bathe will proceed as follows: (1) he will state a contravening view, which in this case is his own – that accidental sharps do not affect the solmization of a passage; (2) he will present three rhetorical *objections* to his view by providing three arguments in support of the opinion that all notes preceded by accidental sharps should be named *mi* (that is, he will present three arguments in support of the third exception); and (3) he will refute each of these arguments in turn, thereby disproving the validity of the third exception and establishing the validity of his own view.

12 In this passage Bathe states his own opinion, contrary to the rhetorical third exception: that accidental sharps do not affect the solmization of a passage.

13 The hypothetical objections that Bathe raises to his assertion that accidental sharps do not affect the solmization of a passage are as follows: (1) no 'sharp' note in the gamut is named *fa*, and therefore no note altered by an accidental sharp should under any circumstances be named *fa*; (2) in the gamut, the distance between *sol* and *fa* is always a whole tone, but the distance between *sol* and an altered pitch named *fa* would be only a semitone; (3) all 'sharp' notes in the gamut are named either *mi* or *la*, and therefore no note altered by an accidental sharp should be named otherwise.

14 Bathe will refute each of the preceding objections by arguing that (1) if the note under *sol* is not allowed to retain its name (*fa*) when it is altered by an accidental sharp but must instead be renamed *mi*, then the syllables *mi* and *fa* would be adjacent in the scale – an arrangement that breaks from the order of the gamut; (2) if the note under *sol* is renamed *mi* when it is altered by an accidental sharp, the syllables would imply that the distance between them would not be a semitone but rather an interval greater than a whole tone; (3) if all notes altered by an accidental sharp are renamed *mi*, situations will arise in which a series of pitches in a musical work (such as B and C♯ when *ut* is G) must be solmized as *mi mi mi*, which would render the syllables useless for the purpose of tuning.

15 Having finished defending his assertion that the appearance of accidental sharps does not affect the solmization of a passage, Bathe turns to the subject of accidental flats. He will proceed as before, according to the principles of *objection and answer*. He will (1) state his own view – that all notes preceded by accidental flats should be named *fa*; (2) raise one hypothetical objection to this view – that renaming notes preceded by flats but not by sharps is inconsistent; and finally (3) 'resolve' this objection by arguing that sharps and flats arise within different musical contexts, and that this fact justifies the different treatment accorded to them by his solmization method. The theoretical implications of his discussion are considered above, pp. 31–32.

16 Throughout Bathe's treatise, the treatment of 'quantitie' and 'time' is so cursory as to be entirely inadequate for the instruction of either proportions or metre. As Rebecca Herissone has observed, his discussion of these subjects seems to reveal the author's awareness 'that mensuration would soon be obsolete' (Herissone, *Music Theory in Seventeenth-Century England*, 28). In any case, it is clear from his treatment

of these topics that Bathe was not particularly interested in them, and that he was far more concerned with the teaching of 'naming' and 'tuning' (that is, solmization) and the instruction of canonic composition than he was with proportion and metre.

[17] If no accidental flats appear in the passage that one wishes to sing, then one may name all of the pitches in the passage according to the 'order of ascension' determined by the presence or absence of signature flats at its beginning.

[18] In order to tune a note altered by an accidental flat, Bathe indicates that one should imagine ('for comptings sake') that both the altered note and the one before it belong to the new 'order of ascension' as indicated by the accidental flat. Having in this way correctly tuned the altered note, one should return to the passage and solmize it in such a way that the syllables reflect the underlying pitch structure of the composition. The actual change of *ut*, in other words, does not occur until the accidental flat first appears. In the example Bathe provides, the singer begins to sing the passage according to the 'order of ascension' with no signature flats and *ut* on G. Then, recognizing that the appearance of the B♭ indicates that a shift to the 'order of ascension' with one flat and *ut* on C has occurred, the singer tunes the whole step between C and B♭ by imagining that the latter 'order' was already in use *before* the accidental flat appeared (thus providing the syllables *sol–fa* for the notes C–B♭). Finally, after having tuned the whole tone between C and B♭ in this manner, the singer resolmizes the passage to reflect the 'orders of ascension' actually employed in the piece. He or she names C as *fa* according to the 'order' with no flats and *ut* on G, and B♭ as *fa* according to the 'order' with one flat and *ut* on C.

[19] In order to tune a note altered by an accidental sharp, Bathe indicates that one should imagine that the passage in which the sharp appears belongs to a (technically non-existent) 'order of ascension' in which *ut* is located a major third below the altered pitch. This enables the singer to tune the semitone between the altered pitch and the one above it as *mi–fa*. After having tuned the altered pitch in this manner (after having 'thus compting by wrong names gotten the right tunes'), the singer should resolmize the passage correctly, in such a way that the appearance of the accidental sharp has no effect on the syllables used. In the example Bathe provides, the singer begins to sing the passage according to the 'order of ascension' with no flats and *ut* on G. Then, in order to tune the semitone between F♯ and G, he or she imagines that *ut* has moved to D, a major third below the altered pitch (thus providing the syllables *fa–mi* for the notes G–F♯). Finally, after tuning the semitone in this manner, the singer resolmizes the passage correctly, naming these notes *sol* and *fa* according to the original 'order of ascension'.

[20] As Bathe's example makes clear, he refers here to the 'order of ascension' with no flats and *ut* on G. His assertion therefore indicates that accidental sharps may appear on F (the 'vpper fa', or seventh degree above *ut*), C (the 'nether fa', or fourth degree above *ut*) or G (the *ut*).

[21] Again referring to the 'order of ascension' with no flats and *ut* on G, Bathe asserts that the appearance of a G♯ in a passage (a 'sharp in the Vt') indicates that both F♯ and C♯ (sharps in the 'vpper fa' and 'nether fa' respectively) should also be sung. His discussion of this point seems to reveal his sensitivity to the fact that accidental sharps were not notated consistently in the music of his time.

[22] As in the previous example, the appearance of a C♯ in a passage (a 'sharp in the nether fa' in the 'order of ascension' with no flats and *ut* on G) indicates that F♯ should also be sung.

[23] Still using the 'order of ascension' with no flats and *ut* on G as the basis for his discussion (as indicated by the example), Bathe explains that flats may be found on B (*mi*) and E (*la*). If a flat is notated on E, the singer must assume that all Bs in the

passage are also to be sung flat. This would in turn imply that the 'order of ascension' with two flats and *ut* on F should be used for tuning.

24   This statement summarizes in a general way Bathe's directives for tuning accidental flats and sharps, both of which require that the singer imagine that a change of *ut* has occurred some time before the actual appearance of the accidental. In the second bar of Bathe's example, the third note should be B♭. Sharps rather than natural signs are provided in Bathe's text.

25   Here Bathe reminds his readers of a point that he made earlier (on sig. Avii[r]) with regard to naming pitches preceded by accidental sharps: that his system is not the only one in use and that the 'cunning singing man' may name the notes of a passage however he likes provided that proper tuning is maintained.

26   In Bathe's text, the thirteenth note of the example is preceded by a sharp rather than a natural sign.

27   Flats cancel sharps, and sharps cancel flats. However, scribes and publishers often fail to provide such directives in their music, thus leaving singers to judge for themselves how long accidental sharps and flats remain in effect.

28   This statement appears to restate and emphasize Bathe's earlier classification of signature flats as B clefs.

29   The last line of music on sig. Biii[v] and the first and last two lines of music on sig. Biv[r] are provided with an indication that they are to be sung in 'Semibrefe time' (see sig. Bi[r]).

30   The harmonization of Psalm 4, 'O God that art my righteousnesse', by Edward Blancks was originally published on pp. 30–31 of Thomas East's *The Whole Booke of Psalmes: With Their Wonted Tunes* (1592). On its appearance in Bathe's treatise, see above, pp. 9–13.

31   Once again Bathe acknowledges that singers may assign a variety of names to the notes of a passage so long as proper tuning is maintained.

32   On Bathe's treatment of 'quantitie' and 'time', see explanatory note 16 above.

33   By *place* Bathe means the interval of imitation. On finding the *place* of a setting, see above, pp. 33–35.

34   Bathe uses the word *course* to describe the piecewise melodic unfolding of the tenor. At each moment of its unfolding, the *course* of the tenor is determined by computing the melodic interval spanned by the tenor across a temporal distance equal to the delay between the initial entrances of the canonic voices. Examples illustrating the computation of the *courses* of a setting are provided above, pp. 33–35.

35   On the use of Bathe's table, see above, pp. 35–40.

36   Bathe provides the following 'figures of obseruation' in order to help his readers avoid some common voice-leading problems that can arise when composing canonic settings at any given *place*. For a discussion of these 'figures', see above, pp. 41–42.

37   On the blade: 'I go where you are, I fall, you see me; help me, Jesus.' On the hilt: 'Add one; remove it; let it stand; add four.'

38   The use of the 'Musical Sword' (*Gladius Musicus*) to compose settings of 'two parts in one' may be summarized as follows:

   In order to find the word on the sword corresponding to the *place* of a setting (the equivalent to finding the column corresponding to the *place* in Bathe's table), the student begins on the word *Aggredior* and moves 'downward' on the blade (towards the hilt) to the second word down (*quo*), which corresponds to the second *place* down; to the third word down (*aderis*), which corresponds to the third *place* down; and so on. For a setting in which the *place* is 'up' rather than 'down', the student begins on the word *Aggredior* and proceeds upward, wrapping around to the hilt, to the second word 'up' (*mi*; the word on the handle, *Ihesu*, is not used), which corresponds to the second *place* up; to the third word up (*adesto*), which corresponds to the third *place* up; and so on.

Then, in order to plot the *course* of the plainsong tenor against the *place* of the setting (the equivalent to finding the square of intersection on Bathe's table), the student begins on the word corresponding to the *place*, turns the sword upside down, and then moves from that word upward or downward along the inverted blade to the word that is the same number of degrees distant as the number of the *course*. In the example considered in Part I of this volume (see pp. 37–42), the *place* was a 'fifth up'. To find the word corresponding to this *place*, the student begins on *Aggredior* and counts 'upward' to *mi* (the second word up, corresponding to the second *place* up), to *adesto* (the third word up, corresponding to the third *place* up), to *cernis* (the fourth word up, corresponding to the fourth *place* up), and finally arrives at *cado* (the fifth word up, corresponding to the *place* up).

Then, in order to plot the intersection of the *place* and the *course*, the student keeps his or her eye on the word *cado* while inverting the sword. Recalling that the first *course* of the setting considered in Part I was a 'second up', the student begins on *cado* and moves up to the second word from *cado* on the inverted sword, and arrives at *cernis*.

Having found the word *cernis*, the student has found the symbolic equivalent of the square of intersection on Bathe's table. In order to interpret the meaning of the compositional directives embodied in the word *cernis*, the student makes note of the vowels that it contains: E and I, the second and fourth vowels alphabetically. This alerts the student to the fact that he or she can begin the leading canonic voice at either a third or a fifth above the tenor (as Bathe explains, the vowel *A* stands for the unison, *E* for the third, *I* for the fifth, and *O* for the sixth).

Continuing with the second *course* of the setting, the student returns to the word *cado* (corresponding to the unchanging *place* a 'fifth up'), inverts the sword (keeps the blade pointing downward), and then counts 'downward' on the inverted sword from *cado* to the second word down, *aderis*. Finding this word (again, the equivalent of finding the square of intersection), the student notes that it contains the vowels A, E and I. He or she thus realizes that the leading canonic voice can be continued on the unison, the third or the fifth above the tenor. The results attained using either of Bathe's graphic devices, the table or the sword, are identical.

[39] 'On Invention': 'Invention grows to infinity in all time, / but it is said that it is often delayed by three evils. / Poverty is a hindrance that prevents inventions from being tested. / The worthless fool says, "It will not be possible". / The lazy man says, "Do you want to walk where the lion is hiding?" / And so, the causes of delay are poverty, silliness and laziness. / Praise now, praise always, praise all the time. / Learning and teaching, speak! And praise be to God.'

[40] This harmonized setting of the psalm 'O Lord in thee is all my trust' by George Kirbye was originally published on pp. 282–85 of Thomas East's *The Whole Booke of Psalmes: With Their Wonted Tunes* (1592). On its appearance in Bathe's treatise, see above, pp. 9–13.

[41] The heading '10. sundry waies of 2. parts in one vpon the plain song.' appears on sig. Cvi[v]–Cviii[v].

PART III

Bathe's *A Briefe Introductione to the True Art of Musicke*: The Extant Text

Andrew Melville's Commonplace Book (University of Aberdeen Library MS 28) and Its Copy of Bathe's 1584 Treatise

The last known extant copy of Bathe's *A Briefe Introductione to the True Art of Musicke* (1584) was the one described in 1776 by Sir John Hawkins in his *General History of the Science and Practice of Music*.[1] As Cecil Hill has noted, two years after the publication of Hawkins's history the historian made a substantial donation of books from his library to the British Museum, and he included in his gift a copy of Bathe's *A Briefe Introduction to the Skill of Song*.[2] We do not know whether this donation included *A Briefe Introductione to the True Art of Musicke*, but the copy he described in 1776 vanished thereafter. Robert Steele included the treatise on a list of 'ghosts' in his 1903 study of English music printing, and for a half-century afterwards the book was all but forgotten by historians.[3] It is therefore as remarkable as it is fortunate that a substantial portion of the text of *A Briefe Introductione to the True Art of Musicke* has since been recovered in the form of a manuscript transcription made in the commonplace book of Andrew Melville (also Andrew Melving or Andro Melvill; 1593–1640), teacher and later master of the Song School at Aberdeen.[4]

It is even more remarkable that Bathe's first treatise should have survived to the present day given that Melville's commonplace book also vanished from public view for more than 70 years and was believed by many Scottish bibliographers to be irretrievably lost. As late as 1886, the book was known to be in the personal library of the London lawyer John Anderson, but its whereabouts were unknown only a decade later and William Walker was compelled to rely on an 1884 manuscript copy of the volume for the preparation of his study *Extracts from the Commonplace Book of Andrew Melville* (1899).[5] Walker, who showed little interest in the musical portions of Melville's book, noted in his study that the volume included among its contents 'ane briefe Introduction to Musick'.[6] He did not, however, include this introduction among the portions of Melville's volume that he published.

Revisiting Walker's study in 1956, Helena Shire suggested that the 'Introduction to Musick' mentioned by Walker might have been Bathe's *A Briefe Introduction to the Skill of Song*. However, since the original commonplace book had been lost and Walker had neglected to include the text of the 'Introduction' in his volume, Shire had little evidence to support her hypothesis at that time.[7] A major breakthrough in her investigation occurred in 1959, just before her essay went to press: the original copy of Melville's commonplace book resurfaced at Sotheby's, where it was bought by the University of Aberdeen. In an appendix added to her study just before publication, Shire argued that the newly available text of the 'briefe Introduction' that had been preserved in Melville's book was not Bathe's *A Briefe Introduction to the Skill of Song* as she had previously suggested, but rather appeared, upon comparison with the description published by Hawkins, to be the lost 1584 treatise.[8] Shire's hypothesis was subsequently confirmed by Hill, who published a transcription of this part of the commonplace book in 1979. A substantial portion of Bathe's text, twice lost, had been recovered.

The source in which large portions of Bathe's text are preserved, Melville's commonplace book (University of Aberdeen Library MS 28), is typical for such volumes in that it contains a miscellaneous assortment of material culled by its owner from a wide variety of sources. Presumably Melville considered some of the material that he copied into his book to be of pedagogical value, but much of it seems to provide a record only of the breadth of Melville's own intellectual curiosity.[9] In the former category, the volume contains, in addition to Bathe's text, 'ane A.B.C.' (an alphabetical rhyme providing moral instruction), a collection of moralizing proverbs and Thomas Ravenscroft's 'The definitions and divisions of moods, tymes, prolationes' (from his *A Briefe Discourse of the True (But Neglected) Vse of Chact'ring the Degrees* [1614]). In the latter category, the volume contains a list of books in Melville's library, the Hebrew alphabet, descriptions of the town clocks (including a transcription, in musical notation, of the 'Toone of the Bells') and a poem by Melville himself.[10]

The transcription that Melville made of Bathe's *A Briefe Introductione to the True Art of Musicke* is both substantial (occupying fols 41^r–52^r of the commonplace book) and meticulous (Melville was careful to preserve the distinction between italic and standard type in the original print; see Figures 3 and 4). As Hawkins's discussion of the treatise reveals, however, the transcription is not complete. Neither the publisher's imprint nor the prefatory discussion cited by Hawkins is preserved in MS 28.[11] This fact, taken together with Cristle Collins Judd's recent observation that commonplace books such as this were typically compiled by excerpting particularly valuable passages, whether large or small, from their original sources,[12] compels us to read the extant text of Bathe's treatise with caution. It is most likely incomplete in a number of respects, many of which cannot be detected in the absence of the original print.

Although Bathe's treatise is only one of two musical texts that Melville copied into his commonplace book, we know from the catalogue that he prepared of books in his library that he owned several music books. In the catalogue itself, Melville accounted for his books only vaguely: 'ane grytt book writtin of the airt of musick', 'ane litle Book of the airt of musick', and so forth. Shire has suggested, however, that Melville's library probably held copies of pedagogical treatises by Morley, Campion and Charles Butler, as well as collections of published music by Morley, John Bull and others.[13] Melville's appointment in 1617 to the post of 'doctor' (instructor) at the Aberdeen Song School – an institution that had already been in existence for nearly 150 years – and his promotion in 1636 to the rank of master of the school testify to the strength of both his training and his skills as a musician.[14]

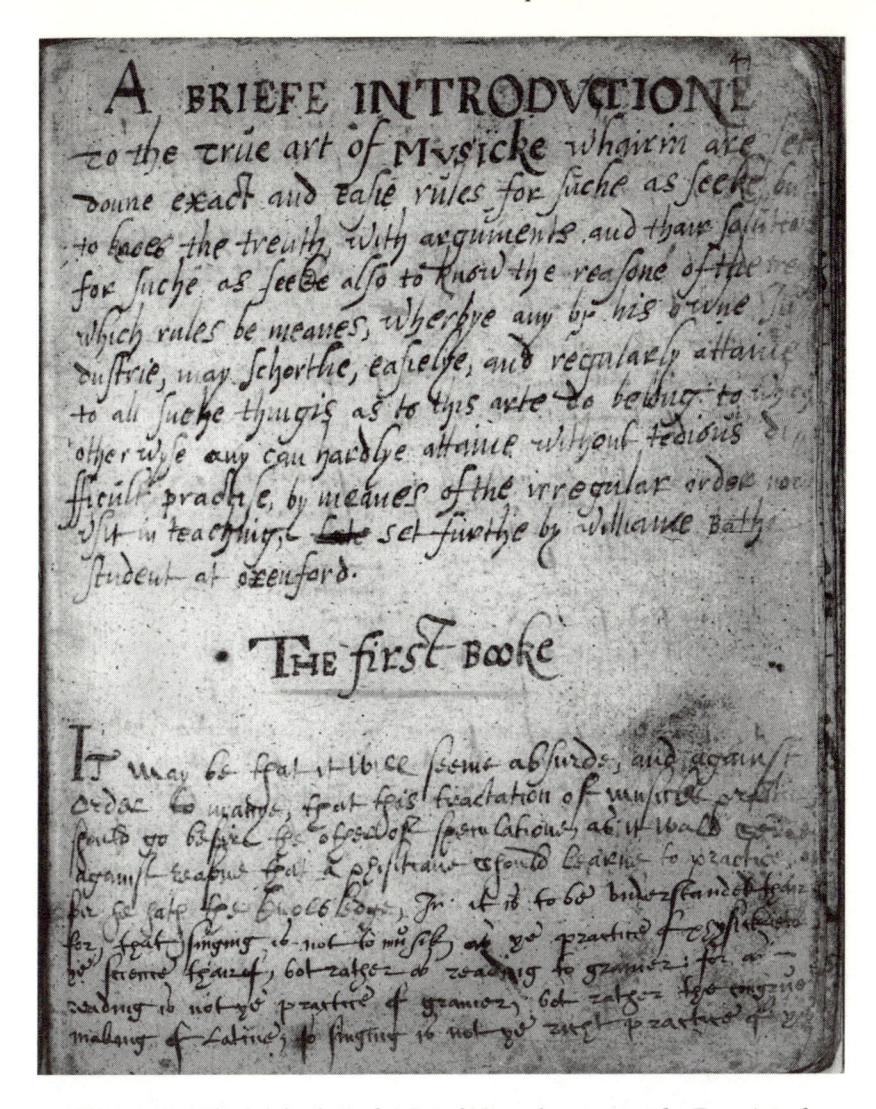

Figure 3 The beginning of *A Briefe Introductione to the True Art of Musicke* in Andrew Melville's Commonplace Book, University of Aberdeen Library MS 28, fol. 41^r

That such a well-read figure as Melville thought highly enough of Bathe's 1584 treatise to copy it painstakingly into his commonplace book only confirms for us the value that Bathe's contributions to music pedagogy were considered to have had by some of his prominent contemporaries.[15]

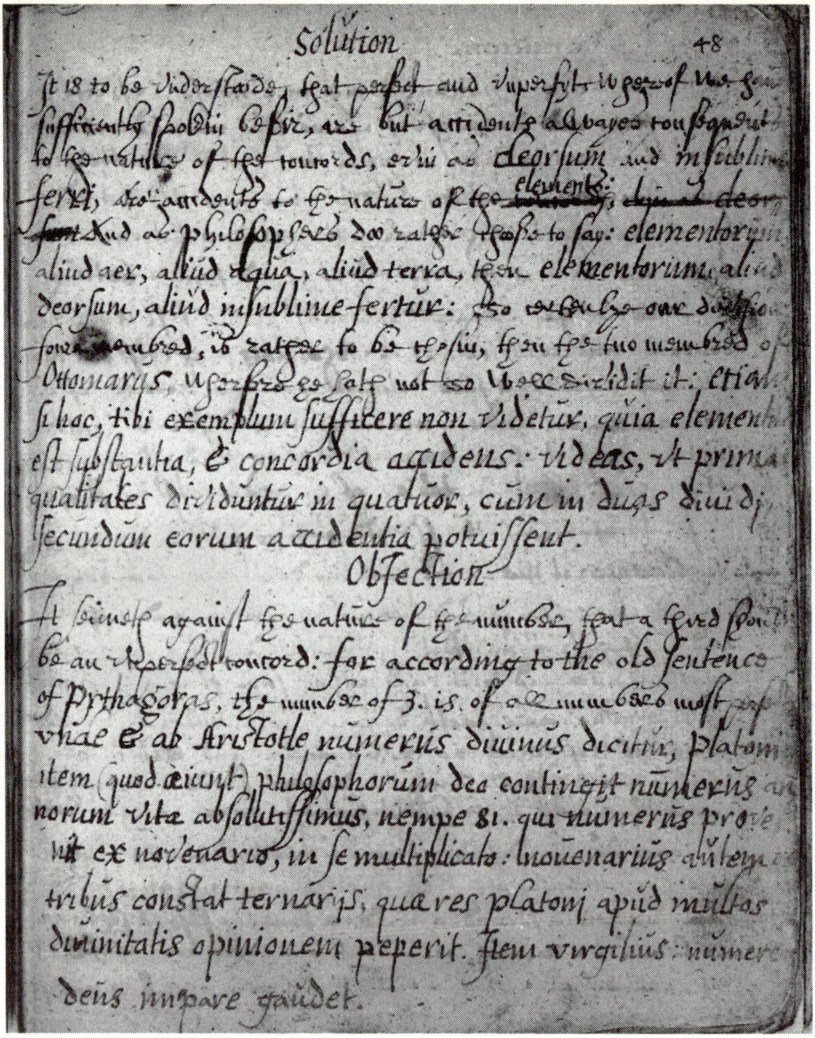

Figure 4 Andrew Melville's Commonplace Book, University of Aberdeen Library MS 28, fol. 48ʳ

It is with this situation in mind, however, that we may once again return to the consideration of Bathe's uncertain legacy with which Part I of this volume concluded. In a collection of songs published in Aberdeen by John Forbes in 1662,[16] we are provided a rare glimpse into the instructional methods employed at the Aberdeen Song School in the period just following Melville's tenure at the institution. Referring on the title page of his collection to the work of

Thomas Davidson, Melville's successor at the school, Forbes advertised the fact that his volume included as a preface 'a briefe Introduction of Musick, As is taught in the Musick-Schole of Aberdene by T.D. *Mr.* of Musick'.[17] This introduction, supposedly supplied by Davidson, includes discussions of the gamut, basic solmization, time and prolation, consonance and dissonance, and ligatures. The preservation of this material in Forbes's volume allows us to assess the degree to which aspects of Bathe's pedagogical methods, which seem to have made such a profound impression upon Melville, persisted in the curriculum at Aberdeen shortly after the latter's death.

Davidson's discussion of the materials of music and solmization is comprised primarily of unattributed quotations not from Bathe's work but from Morley's *Plaine and Easie Introduction to Practicall Musicke*. The only passage in Davidson's introduction that might be considered even remotely indebted to Bathe is found in his discussion of the gamut, but even here Davidson merely plagiarizes a passage from Morley's text that Jessie Ann Owens has identified as possibly originating in Bathe's *A Briefe Introduction to the Skill of Song*.[18] If Davidson's introduction does indeed reflect the pedagogical practices employed at the Song School in the mid-seventeenth century, then Bathe's work seems to have made no lasting impression upon them.

Relationship between the Treatises

As in the case of *A Briefe Introduction to the Skill of Song*, the modern reception of *A Briefe Introductione to the True Art of Musicke* seems to have suffered unfairly from the taint of Hawkins's comments.[19] Writing sarcastically in his *General History* on the relationship between the two treatises, Hawkins remarked that 'how highly soever the author might value his own work [that is, the 1584 treatise], he thought proper some years after the first publication to write it over again in such sort, as hardly to retain a single paragraph of the former edition'.[20] More than a hundred years after Hawkins's comments were published, and even after the appearance of Hill's edition of portions of *A Briefe Introductione to the True Art of Musicke* in 1979, scholars have tended to follow Hawkins's lead in assessing the relationship between the two volumes; they have continued, as Owens notes, 'to regard the second treatise as a "wholesale revision" of the first'.[21]

Owens, who appears to have been the first to examine the relationship between the two volumes critically, observes that they may more accurately be described as 'two separate treatises, with some overlap in content'.[22] This is in fact an accurate assessment of the relationship. As discussed in Part I of this volume, *A Briefe Introduction to the Skill of Song* includes a large amount of material borrowed directly from *A Briefe Introductione to the True*

Art of Musicke. All of the borrowed material, however, is confined to the first part of the 1596 text: to the section 'For Naming' in 'The ante rules of Song'. The remainder of *A Briefe Introduction to the Skill of Song* – the bulk of the treatise – is comprised of newly composed material. In turn, most of the text of *A Briefe Introductione to the True Art of Musicke*, including the extensive discussions of consonance and counterpoint transcribed on fols 45^v–52^r of Melville's book, was not reused by Bathe.

In examining the relationship between the treatises, it is particularly illuminating to consider the ways in which the transfer of material from the earlier treatise into the later volume took place. Significantly, it was neither simple nor direct. Rather, some of the material originally published in the 1584 treatise was set apart from the rest of the text of *A Briefe Introduction to the Skill of Song* by the heading 'The Rule of Vt', and was provided with a more detailed explication in the later volume than in the earlier book. It may be that the transformation of this early material into 'The Rule of Vt' can provide us with insight into the process by which the central theory underlying Bathe's solmization method developed in the author's mind during the mid-1580s.

Towards the beginning of his discussion of 'naming' pitches in *A Briefe Introductione to the True Art of Musicke*, Bathe first made note of the fact that the location of *ut* can be determined by the presence or absence of signature flats in the passage to be sung (fol. 43^r in Melville's book). By the time he set down to write *A Briefe Introduction to the Skill of Song*, his conception of this issue had changed subtly, yet in a way that was to have a profound impact on his own assessment of his solmization method. Significantly, at some point between 1584 and the time when he completed his second treatise, Bathe had come to recognize the signature flat as a B clef. This broadening of his conception of clef allowed him to provide his readers with a method for finding the location of *ut* that required them to consider only a single feature of the passage to be tuned: the clef or combination of clefs that appears at its beginning.[23]

In *A Briefe Introduction to the Skill of Song*, Bathe labelled his entire discussion of the relationship between signature flats and the location of *ut* – much of which was taken directly from his 1584 treatise – as 'The Rule of Vt'. He also provided his readers with eight examples of its application, none of which had appeared in the earlier book. As I have argued in Part I of this volume, it was Bathe's elaboration of his earlier observations into the single, comprehensive directive called 'The Rule of Vt' that enabled him to outline a non-hexachordal solmization method that allowed for the tuning of accidental sharps and flats. It may have been this very elaboration, moreover, that prompted him to write his 1596 treatise in the first place. While *A Briefe Introductione to the True Art of Musicke* was a typical late sixteenth-century primer, treating the materials of music in its first section and rudimentary composition in its second, *A Briefe Introduction to the Skill of Song* is, as its title suggests, primarily concerned with teaching novice musicians to sing. And Bathe's most important contribution to the area of singing pedagogy was, as he himself declared, his 'Rule of Vt'. By examining the relationship between the treatises, we therefore catch a glimpse of the evolution of Bathe's singing method, and of his own later discovery of the profound significance of an earlier observation. The passages cited below constitute the complete text shared by the volumes.

A Briefe Introductione to the True Art of Musicke (1584), transcribed in University of Aberdeen Library MS 28, fols 42^r–43^r

A Briefe Introduction to the Skill of Song (c.1596), sig. Av^r–Avi^v

[fol. 42^r] and *G* cleif is ye mark of ye higher *G sol re vt* in ye scalle: & the *C:* cleif of yat place called *c sol fa vt* and ye *F* cleif [fol. 42^v] of *F fa vt* the lower in the scale.

[sig. Av^r] The *G:* cliefe is the mark of the higher *G sol re vt*. In the scale: & the *C:* clefe of that placed called *C sol fa vt*. And the *F:* cliefe of *F fa vt* the lower in the scale.

Now in this sort you maye find by the cleife where everye note standeth and least their should seime any difficultie, I will begin from the first secht of the booke, that all things that doe belonge to thair knowledge, may be better wnderstood. First when a man seeth the booke befoir him he may see certaine rules which go along lineallye by 5. and by 5. whiche number of 5. in called a set of prick song (for a sett of plainesong hath com*m*onlye but 4. rules), then he may see in the first of the set alwayes one of the foirsaid cleifes wpon some rule, and whatsoever note standeth wpone the same rule, with the cleife, is said to be in that place whairofe that cleife whiche he seeth is the marke. Iff any note stande in the next space aboue, it is said to stand in the next place aboue that place whereof that cleife is the marke, and so wpward and donward continuallye counting from the close as in this example.

Now in this sort you may finde by the cliefe where euery note standeth: and least there should seeme any difficultie, I will begin from the first sight of the booke, that all things that doe belong to their knowledge, may bee the better vnderstoode. First when a man seeth the booke before him he may see certaine rules which goe along lineally by 5 and 5 which number of 5 is called a set of pricksong (for a set of plainesong hath commonly but 4. rules,) then he may see in the first of the set always one of the foresayde cleifes vpon some rule, and whatsoeuer note standeth vpon the same rule with the cliefe, is said to be in that place whereof that cleife which [sig. Av^v] he seeth is the marke, and if any note stand in the next space aboue, it is said to stand in the next place aboue that place, whereof that cleife is the marke. And so vpward and downeward continually counting from the close as in this example.

[example]

[example]

The first note standeth in *c sol fa vt*, becaus it standeth wpon the same rule with the cleife which is the marke of *c sol fa vt*, The second in *D la sol re*, becaus *d la sol re* is next aboue *C sol fa vt* in the scale of *gam vt*, The Thrid in *b fa ♮ mi* Becaus it is the nixt place beneath *C sol fa vt*, the fourth in *e la mi* because elami is the nixt place saue one to csolfavt, and ye said fourth note standeth in ye next place saue one to the cleife whiche is the marke of the place q^t *c sol fa vt* is, and so of all the other notes: then in the end of the lyn or sett, he may see a thing marked thus

The first note standeth in *C sol fa vt*, because it standeth vpon the same rule with the clief which is the mark of *C sol fa vt*, the second in *D la sol re*, because *D la sol re* is next aboue *C sol fa vt* in the scale of *Gam vt*: the third in *B fa b mi*, because it is in the next place beneath *C sol fa vt*: the fourth in *E la mi*, because *E la mi* is the next place saue one to *C sol fa vt*, & the said fourth note standeth in the next place saue one to the cliefe which is the mark of the place *C sol fa vt*. And so of all other notes: then in the ende of the set, hee may see a thing thus

[example]

[example]

which is called a director, Becaus it is always put wpon the rule or space wherin the first of the next lyn or sett standeth, and doth so direct a man, evin as in bookes the word that is lowest wpon everye of the leafe doth direct a man to the word nixt following:

marked, which is called a direct, because it is always put vpon the rule or space wherein the first of the next set standeth, and doth so direct a man, euen as in bookes the word that is lowest vpon euery side of the leafe doth direct a man to the word next following.

The rule of Vt.

[fol. 43^r] The third that is necessery to be knowin for the Richt naming of notes, is the place whair yat note standeth whiche is named *vt*. and as by counting vpward and dounwarde from the cleife it is knowen where every note standeth, so it is knowin by counting wpward and dounward from that which is callit *vt*, quhat the Richt name of everie note is: Bot first let us set downe how ye place Whair

The next thing necessary to be knowne for the right naming of notes, is the place where that note standeth which is named *Vt*. And as by counting vpward and downeward from the cliefe it is to bee knowne where euery note standeth, so it is to be knowne by counting vpward and downeward from that which is called *Vt*, what the right name of euery note is: but first let vs set downe how the

Relationship between the Treatises 109

the *vt* standeth is knowin, which is thus, there be three places, in one of whiche the *vt* must alwayes be: that is to say in *G*. which is *Gam vt* and *g sol re vt*. Quhan thair is no flat in *C* whiche is *C fa vt*, *C sol fa vt*, and *C sol fa*, quhane thair is a flat in ♯ *mi*, or *b fa* ♯ *mi*, In *F* Whiche is *f fa vt*, when thair ar to flats, one in *b fa* ♯ *mi*, the other in *e la mi*.

As for example

[example]

place where the *vt* standeth is knowen, [sig. Avi^r] which is thus. There be three places, in one of which the *vt* must alwaies be: that is to say, in *G*, which is *Gamvt* and *G sol re vt*, when there is no flat in *C*, which is *C fa vt*, *C sol fa vt*, and *C sol fa*, when there is a flat in *b mi*, or *b fa b mi*. In *F* which is *F fa vt*, when there are two flats, one in *b mi* or *b fa b mi*, the other in *E la mi*, or *E la*.

As for example.

[example]

¶No b flat, the *(vt)* in G. The b flat in b onely, the *(vt)* in C. The b flat in b and E, the *(vt)* in F.

1   G putteth V to the same place.
2
3   F. and B. to the next vp, as.

[example]

4   C putteth *Vt* to the fift place vp, and from C down to the fourth. B, taketh place of the rest. B, is placed last to shew that it taketh place of the rest.
5   If there commeth two, b.b. being a fourth, the vpper taketh place.
6   And being a fift, the nether taketh place, as:

[example]

[sig. Avi^v]
7   D. putteth *Vt* to the fift place down, but it is sedome vsed.
8   If there commeth two b.b. being a second a sunder, the lower

When Yow haue in this sort found out the *vt*, you must wnderstand that everye note that standeth in the nixt place to that is *re* if it go wpward, the nixt is *mi*, the nixt *fa*, the *sol*, then *la*, ascending vp alwayes orderlye counting the rules, and spaces:

and as Ye ascend *wt. re. my. fa. sol. la. fa.*

so dounward lykwayes, *fa. la. sol. fa. my. re. vt.* and so come to fa a gaine. and In sorte the richt name of everie note is knawen. Two things from thes rules are excepted, the on is that everye *re.* should be named *la*, when Yow ascend to it, or descend from it, and that everie *vt*, should be named *sol*, whiche tuo things ar wsed *euphoniæ gratia*, and yet this name *vt* is most proper to the Bas. or lowest parte in the first place.

taketh place, which chanceth very rare.

More shall be sayd of naming in the chapter of tuning.

When you haue in this sort found out the *vt*, you must vnderstand that euery note that standeth in the next place aboue it is named *re*, euery note that standeth in the next place to that is named *mi*, in the next to that *fa*, then *sol*, then *la*, then *fa*, ascending vp alwaies orderly, counting the rules, and spaces: then next aboue that againe is *vt*: for you shall finde that place, which is the eight place from that wherein your other *vt* stood, to begin with the same letter: So that if the rules & spaces were infinite, you might in this manner giue euey note his right name: and as you did count vpward *Vt, re, mi, fa, sol, la, fa*, and so come againe to *vt*: so must you come downeward from *vt*, the same way backward, by *fa, la, sol, fa, mi, re, vt*. And so come to *fa*, againe. And in this sort the right name of euery note is knowne. Two things from these rules are excepted, the one is, that euery *re*, should be named *la*, when you ascend to it, or descend from it: and that euery *vt*, should bee named *sol*, which two things are vsed *euphoniæ gratia*, and yet this name of *vt*, is most proper to the base or lowest part in the first place.

Editorial Note

The transcription of Bathe's *A Briefe Introductione to the True Art of Musicke* that follows attempts to present as accurately as possible the full extant text of the treatise. This text is preserved in three sources, all of which are incomplete with respect to the original print: Andrew Maunsell's *Catalogue of English Printed Bookes* (1595), which preserves the text of the title page only;[24] Hawkins's *A General History of the Science and Practice of Music*, which preserves the title page, publisher's imprint and a portion of the preface;[25] and University of Aberdeen Library MS 28, which preserves all of the extant text except the publisher's imprint and preface (fols. 41^r–52^r). Unless noted otherwise in square brackets, the source for the transcription is University of Aberdeen Library MS 28. In the case of the single passage from Bathe's text that is preserved in all three sources (the title page), all discrepancies between the sources are noted except those deriving solely from Melville's use of a Scottish system of spelling. The present transcription differs in only minor respects from Hill's 1979 edition.

The present transcription has been prepared following the general guidelines outlined in Preston and Yeandle's *English Handwriting 1400–1650*.[26] The spelling and diction used in the relevant source, whether rendered by Hawkins, Melville or Maunsell, is maintained with three exceptions: where a tilde appears over a letter in the original, indicating the need to supply an 'm' or an 'n' immediately afterwards, the missing 'm' or 'n' is supplied in a contrasting typeface (in italics when the word is transcribed in roman type, in roman type when the word is transcribed in italics); superior letters have been lowered tacitly; and missing letters have been supplied in italics. Angled brackets (< >) indicate crossed out passages. Wherever possible, the formatting of the original manuscript has also been maintained. In addition, the transcription of material from Melville's volume maintains, to the extent possible, the scribe's careful distinction between Secretary and Italic hand (see Figures 3 and 4). In the present transcription, Secretary hand has been rendered with italics and Italic hand with standard type. Although this may be the opposite of Melville's intended effect (it seems likely that he used the Italic hand to convey the emphasis of italic type in the original print, defaulting to the more informal Secretary hand for the bulk of his copying), this choice has been made in order to preserve as closely as possible the appearance of the manuscript.

112   *A Briefe Introductione to the True Art of Musicke,* Part III

Transcription

[fol. 41ʳ]

A BRIEFE INTRODVCTIONE

To the True art of Mvsicke *whairin are set doune exact and easie rules*[a] *for suche as seeke but to know the treuth, with arguments and thair solutions for suche as seeke also to know the reasone of treuth,*[b] *which rules be meanes, wherbye any by his owne Industrie, may schortlie, easielye, and regularly attaine to all suche thingis as to this arte do belong: to which otherwyse any can hardlye attaine without tedious difficult practise, by meanes of the irregular order now usit in teaching, late*[c] *set furthe by Williame Bathe student at oxenford.*

[Hawkins, p. 497]
Imprinted at London by Abel Jeffes, dwelling in Sermon-lane neere Paules Chaine, anno 1584.[d]

being rhetorically persuaded to graunt to the publishing therof, I forbore to do it till I had considered two thinges, whereof the one was the worthinesse of the matter. The other, the feeding of the common affections. But for the worthinesse, I thought it not to be doubted, seeing heere one set forth a booke of a hundred mery tales;[e] another of the battaile between the spider and the fly;[f] another De Pungis Porcorum; another of a monster born at London the second of January, hedded lyke a horse and bodied lyke a man, with other such lyke fictions; and thinking this matter then some of these to be more worthy. As for the other, wich is to feede the common affections of the patient learned, I doubt not but it may soon be; but he that wil take in hand to serve to the purpose of every petty pratler, may as soone by sprinckling water suffice the drienes of the earth, as bring his purpose to passe.

---

[a] After *rules*, Maunsell has '*with Arguments, and their Solutions, for such as seeke* …'.

[b] Maunsell has *the truth*; Hawkins has *the treuth*.

[c] *late* crossed out in MS 28; Hawkins has *lately*.

[d] Hawkins notes that the treatise included a dedication to Bathe's uncle Gerald Fitzgerald, Earl of Kildare; he does not, however, cite the text of this dedication (Hawkins, *A General History of the Science and Practice of Musick*, 497).

[e] Hawkins notes: 'The author here means a translation of Les Centes Nouvelles nouvelles, which is mentioned by Ames to have been printed about this time. The original was published in 1455, by Louis XI. of France, then dauphin, during his retreat from his father's court to that of the duke of Burgundy' (ibid.).

[f] Hawkins notes: 'The Parable of the Spider and the Fly, quarto, 1556, in old English verse, by John Heywood' (ibid.).

[fol. 41ʳ]

THE *first Booke*

IT *may be that it will seeme absurde, and against order to manye, that this tractation of musicke practice should go befoir the other of speculatione, as it would semme against reasone that a phisitiane should learne to practice befoir he hath the knowledge, In it is to be vnderstanded thair for, that singing is not to musik, as ye practice of physick is to ye science thairof, bot rather as reading to gramer: for as – reading is not ye practice of gramer, bot rather the congrue making of Latine, so singing is not ye richt practice of ye* [fol. 41ᵛ] *practice of ye richt speculationne of musick, but rather artificicall setting is ye speculatione: and as by guid ordour reading must goe befoir gramer, so it var not against ordr, that singing soud go befor setting, although the on may be had vithout ye vther inso much as a not is the thing that is must matiriallie intreated of in all the first book, and as it var ye subiect of this former part called,* ars cantandi, *to quhich the naming, tyme, quantitie, &c. doth be long: it var not vnfit thairof to giw sume apart descreptionne, vharby ye natur of it micht be ye better knawen,*

of quhich { A not is a sound tuned *som be naturall, as is sounded bye ye voice of a living creature: sum artificicall, as is plaid vpon instrumentes.*

to notis belong four things, quhich being knaven, doe yeild the perfect skill and knav- ledge of song that is to say the richt – { *naming. quantitie tyme tune*

<For the richt naming> *For the richt naming*
Albeit that ye skilfull singing man; keiping evrie not in his richt tune, may name it at his pleasour, never ye les, a learner sould heardlie come to that perfectionne, vith out learning to nam tham aricht befor; it is thairfor to be vnderstanded that ther be bot sax severall names – that is, vt, re, mi, fa, soll, la, and the deficultie lyith in knaving vhether ye sax severall names ar to be atribut to evrie note: for ye solvtionne of quich deficultie, ther ar things neceassarie to be knaven, vherof, ye first is the scale of (gam vt) the secund is to be knaven in what place [fol. 42ʳ] evrie not standeth, the third to knav in quhat plac yat not standeth quihch is named .vt. By the knavledg and remembrance, of thes thrie, the name of any not may be knaven, as I vill schav hereftor, let us first therfor orderlie set down the schall of :gam vt: vhich is so named becaus :gam vt: is ye lowest plac, and as it var ye foundationn in that scalle quhich is yus commonlie placed –

114   *A Briefe Introductione to the True Art of Musicke*, Part III

E la	G sol re vt	B fa b my	D sol re
De la sol	F fa vt	A la mi re	C fa vt
C sol fa	E la my	G sol re vt	B my
B fa b my	D la sol re	F fa vt	A re
A la mi re	C sol fa vt	E la my	Gam vt

quhat *is be neath* gesolrevt, *is beneath* .gam vt. *during four.* & quhat *is aboue* elamy, *may be immagined or set doun aboue* Ela; *The secund thing that is to be knaven, as I said befor, is in what place of ye former scalle evrie not standeth; for ye knavledg of quhich, seing it is knaven by the cleif, it var nessasrie to knav* <illegible text crossed out> *quhat a cleif is; quhich is nothing else bot a mark of on of these places contened in the scalle of* gam vt, *quharby it is knaven in* quhat *place evrie not standeth: quharof ther be thrie kyndes commonlie vsed, yat is to say* –

{ G sol re vts
  C sol fa vts
  F fa vts }   *quhich are thuse marked*   { G or thus
                                              C or thus
                                              F or thus }

and G *cleif is ye mark of ye higher* G sol re vt *in ye scalle:* & *the* C: *cleif of yat place called* c sol fa vt *and ye* F *cleif* [fol. 42ᵛ] *of* F fa vt *the lower in the scale.*

Now in this sort you maye find by the cleife where everye note standeth: and least their should seime any difficultie, I will begin from the first secht of the booke, that all things that doe belonge to thair knowledge, may be ye better wnderstood. First when a man seeth the booke befoir him he may see certaine rules which go along lineallye by 5. and by 5. whiche number of 5. is called a set of prick song (for a sett of plainesong hath commonlye but 4. rules), then he may see in the first of the set always one of the foirsaid cleifes wpon some rule, and whatsoever note standeth wpone the same rule, with the cleife, is said to be in that place whairofe that cleife whiche he seeth is the marke. Iff any note stande in the next space aboue, it is said to stand in the next place aboue that place whereof that cleife is the marke, and so wpward and donward continuallye counting from the close as in this example

The first note standeth in c sol fa vt, *becuas it standeth wpon the same rule with the cleife which is the marke of* c sol fa vt, *The second in* D la sol re, *becaus* d la sol re *is next aboue* C sol fa vt *in the scale of* gam vt, *The Thrid in* b fa ♮ mi *Becaus it is the nixt place beneath* C sol fa vt, *The fourth in* e la mi *because elami is the nixt place saue one to csolfavt, and ye said fourth note standeth in ye next place saue one to the cleife whiche is the marke of the place* quer c sol fa vt *is, and so of all the other notes: Then in the end of the lyn or sett, he may see a thing marked thus*

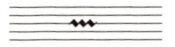

which is called a director, Becaus it is always put wpon the rule or space wherin the first of the next lyn or sett standeth, and doth so direct a man, evin as in bookes the word that is lowest wpon everye of the leafe doth direct a man to the word nixt following:

[fol. 43ʳ]

 The third that is necessery to be knowin for the Richt naming of notes, is the place whair yat note standeth whiche is named vt. *and as by counting vpward and dounwarde from the cleife it is knowen where every note standeth, so it is knowin by counting wpward and dounward from that which is callit* vt, *quhat the Richt name of everie note is: Bot first let us set downe how ye place Whair the* <illegible text crossed out> vt *standeth is knowin, which is thus, there be three places, in one of whiche the* vt *must alwayes be: that is to say in* G. *whiche is* Gam vt *and* g sol re vt. *Quhan thair is no flat in* C *whiche is* C fa vt, C sol fa vt, *and* C sol fa, *quhane thair is a flat in* ♮ mi, *or* b fa ♮ mi, *In* F *Whiche is* f fa vt, *when thair ar to flats, one in* b fa ♮ mi, *the other in* e la mi.

As for example

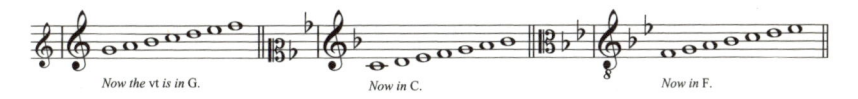

When Yow haue in this sort found out the vt, *you must wnderstand that everye note that standeth in the nixt place to that is* re *if it go wpward, the nixt is* mi, *the nixt* fa, *the* sol, *then* la, *ascending vp alwayes orderlye counting the rules, and spaces: and as Ye ascend* wt. re. mi. fa. sol. la. fa. *so dounward lykwayes,* fa. la. sol. fa. mi. re. vt. *and so come to fa againe. and In sorte the richt name of everie note is knawen. Two things from thes rules are excepted, the on is that everye* re. *should be named* la, *when Yow ascend to it, or descend from it, and that everie* vt, *sould be named* sol, *whiche tuo things ar wsed* euphoniæ gratia, *and yet this name* vt *is most proper to the Bas. or lowest parte in the first place.*

116 *A Briefe Introductione to the True Art of Musicke,* Part III

[fol. 43ᵛ]
For the quantitie

Next to the richt naming of the notes, according to the former devisione followeth the quantitie, quhiche is the length of the note: according to the diversitie of whiche it is divided into eight kynds as followes

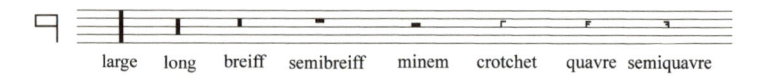

large long breiff semibreiff minem crotchet quavre semiquavre

heir is to Be notted, that a pricke put after any note doth cause the note going befoir it to be halfe so long againe as it is of it selff

For the Tyme

Next to the quantitie according to the former divisione followeth the tyme, whiche Tyme is a measouring of the former quantities, schewed to learners, By stricking the hand or foote of quhiche thair be tuo kynds, that is to say semibreiff tym, and thrie minem tyme, By tym Yow must learne how long Yow sould hold one of the former quantities, in thair due measoures, for the just lenth of the Tyme it selff, thair can be no certaintie, for it is according to the singers pleasour, etheir to Begin with a slow tym, or a fast, so that the same Tym that is begune be oberued to the end, The tyme is a certene thing wher we do measour the quantitie of nottes: for albeit the nottes haue a certane quantitie everie on, yet it is not knowen how long this certaintie should Be, without the Tyme, wheirfor the tyme is the certentie of each quantitie, and
[fol. 44ʳ] *Theirfoir may weill be called a measoure: And this is a gen to Be obserued concerning the semibreiff Tyme, that Yow must pute of the notes, as many as mak wp the length of the minem, to the putting down of the hand, and as many as mak wp of the length of ane other minem to the taking doune of the hand In this kynd of Tyme.*

 The other kynd of tyme called thrie minem tyme, doth in this differ frome the other, that the former tyme is alwayes the length of a semibreiff: And this kynd of Tyme called thre minem tyme, is first the length of a semibreiff, and then of a minem, <And this kynd of Tyme you must measour first putting wp and doune your hand> and this Tyme ar all galliardes measoured,

For the tune

The richt names, the quantities, and tymes being knawn, it now followeth, that we should tell of tuing the voice, wherby the reight tunes of the notes ar knawn the order of tuning the woice is, that the keiping of tune in lifting wp and falling downe of ye voic should be according as the Notes doe stand, either in one place, ascending, or descending in the rules and spaces, for the good obseruation of tuning the woice, it wer best to sing the first not as Yow think most agreiabl to your woice: then if the next not be in the next rule or space abowe, lett the woice be lifted wp one nott, if it be in the next sawe one, let the voice be lifted wp twa notes: likwisse, if the next not be beneath: and soe down or wpward, according as the notes ar distant. Ther ar twa thingis to be noted as exceptions from these precedent rules, wherof ye on is. that from e la mi, and everie place wher any sharp is, [fol. 44ᵛ] *which is thus marked ♯ To the nixt note aboue it, the voice should be altered but halff a note, the other that in descending from fa, or any note that hath a scharpe befoir the nixt note wnder it, the voice sould lykwayes be altered but halff a note, if I sould leave this Tractatione in this sort, telling that suche a tyme the voice must be lifted vp a note, and suche a tyme halff a note, I sould yet leave a great difficultie to the young learner to know when the voice is liftit vp halfe a note, and quen a whole note: for to know this doth requyre Tyme and experience, neverthes the best way is to exercise ascending and descending orderlye as in this example.*

Obiection

The concord called a fyft, doth consist of fyue notes in distance, for so it appeareth by the denomination, that their foir it is called a fyft, and thair is a fyft in con[g] *concord betuixt* <illegible text crossed out> */a/ and h. vpon the stoped Instrument, such as ane lute or siterne, Thairfoir Thairfoir*[h] *thair sould be five notes in distance, whiche in deed by this former compting is not, and consequentlye, etheir a fyft doth not consist of fyue notes, whiche is contrary to the denomination, or this former compting is naught.*

Solution

Their ar 2. kindis of distance, one betwext the places that ar put down in the scale of Gam vt, ane other betwext notes [fol. 45ʳ] *Themselues, according to the former acount: and the destance wherof concordis haue ther denomination, is betwext the places of Gam vt: and ewerie fift (that is a concord) according to This account, oucht to los according to the other account, half a not: and ewerie 8. according to this account, in Gam vt, oucht to los a whol not, according to the orther account.*

---

[g] Transcribed as in original.
[h] *Thairfoir* repeated in MS 28.

Replication

It is said in this letter solutionn, that ewerie fift according To the places of Gamut, *that is according (as though som fifth wer no concorde) which when it may not be, thes words ar superfluous.*

Resolutione

It may be in some, that a fift according to the places aforesaid may Be a discord, as vhen the one is flat, and the other sharp: & the reasone why this fift as others, is no concorde is, that according to the other account, it loseth mair then half a Not, which it should not do (as I said before) heir is to be noted, that 2 nots and a half according to the other account maketh a third according to this: as when on standeth in a la mi re, *the other being in* C sol fa vt. *Bot of this moir at lairg in ther owen places. Let it not seime strang to any, that I haue not maid mention of the diuersitie of moods and proportiones in this place: for I haue omited them for 2. causes: the one is, that other moods, then that which by thes that be heir may be wnderstood, ar not now commonlye vsed, and moreour it wald breid great tediousness. and if any wher they chanc, he that knoweth thes that be heir, may by declaration of fewe words vnder* [fol. 45^v] *stand them. as for the proportions, ther be of them so many kindis, that it would goe neir to tak vp againe, as much as this book, to intreat of them at lairg: ye other is: that of thes 4 thinges, wherin the knowledg of singing dooth consist. that is to say, reicht naming, quantitie, tym, and order of the voic: the proportione differ but in one, that is to say, in quantitie, therfor to mak a long tractation of them may be thought vain he that will for the naming, quantitie, tym, and order of woice, obserue thes ruls aforesaid, may with little practis sing at the frist sicht. also he that will keip well in mynd the way to find out ye thrie vts, may soone perceiwe when any Ignorant clairk playeth wilde voluntarie: that is to say, when he begineth (vt being in gam vt) and endeth with vt in* f fa vt *or* C sol fa vt, *whiche is allowed as his ansuer, that being demanded the way to londone: saide a bag full of plumes.*

sic finit ars cantandi.

Laus nunc, laus semper, laus omni tempore summa
Discens atque docens, dicite, lausque Deo.

THE second booke

IT *now followeth that sould speake of musick speculative,* querin great pleasure *may be had, whiche also may worthily be numbred among the* 7. liberall sciences, *And first of the concord betwixt pairts. Then orderly as it shall seeme most fit for the easie* Intro [fol. 46ʳ] Introductione *of the learner: wherein if there seeme any doubt we will with gods grace, as heirtofore we haue done, with objections and thair solutions make it plaine, and in some places also schew the opinions of the learned and then after put Doune what is most probable and most worthie to be accepted.*

Becaus *that a concord is the thing that is most mentioned In all this tractation, as in knowing the number of them, The placing and making of them, it wer not wnfit first to Declare the natuure of it, Then by diuisione to declare the number of them,* And *as for the nature of it, It must be wnderstoode that a concord is an agreement of tuo or mo pairts. The common division is thus.*

A concord is divided into an	{	Vnizon Third Fyft Sixt Eighth Tenth Twelth Thirtenth and a Fyftenth

The *difficulty of this division schall by objections be made plain.*

Objection

Thes concords numbered, an vnizon, a thrid, &c. which the logicians call, membra diuidentia, *doth not containe as much as a concord, which they call Diuisiuns, therfor the diuisione is Naught: for a seuenth[i] with many more, which ar not heir contayned ar concordes.*

[fol. 46ᵛ]

<Objection> Solution

Thogh not expresly, yet in maner of reductione they ar contained for a seuententh to a Third, becaus it is a concord of that kynd and a ninetenth to a fift lykwayes is reduced.

---

[i] As noted in Hill (p. 12 n. 10), *seventeenth* must be intended.

Replication

Then it is naught for another cause, that is to say, because it containeth more then richt: for by that solution I may say, that ther ar but 4. concordes, because all the other numbres, ar reduced to one of the first 4. as a seuententh and a nyntenth ar: for an eyght to an vnizon: a tenth to a third: a twelfth to a fift: a thirtenth to a sixt: a fifteenth againe to ane vnizon are reduced.

Resolutione

I cannot in very deed, by giuing a solution to this last argument defend this diuision to be logical, as it should be indeid: for the precepts that ar taught in logick of a division doe not onlye belong to the same science. Neverthiles, for a solutione, I will schew the caus, why this divisione hath Bein so long accepted; It is to be wnderstode theirfoir That long tyme after the Invention of musicke Thair wer but tuo partes vsed, or at the most 3. as apeireth by ancient wreitters, and Becaus that for that number of pairtes this number of concordes did suffice, it was acceptit, netheir do I think notwithstanding But they knew that ther were moir concordes: But They saw withall: that how farsoevere they had [fol. 47r] *numbered, they should haue left more to be numbered.*

Then after there grew great diversitie in opinions among musitianes, of this division, as concerning the number of concordes: for Berhusius[j] *in dividing the concords accepteth the common divisione, and sayth That their is a great Contentione, Betuixt musitianes, of The number of concords, Bot for his solutione, the difficultie yet remaineth, Also* ottomarus lucinius argentinus,[k] *In The first chapter of his second commentarie, devideth the concords in this sort: Thair be tuo kyndes of concords,* perfect *and* vnperfect: *perfect ar ane vnizon, a fyft, and suche as are to them reduced: To ane Vnizon are reduced ane eight, a fiftenth and a tuo and tuentith: to a fyft are reduced a tuelth a nyntenth, Wnperfyt are suche as haue affinitie uith the Thrid, and sixt, as a tenth a thretenth a sevententh, and twentith: also he sayth That they are called perfect, becaus they doe end songs: saying:* Eo quod omne carmen per longas ambages profectum tandem in his finem quæritat, *nether doth this divisione please me, albeit it seemeth to be more artificiall then the common divisione, for that it wer more fit, to divide a concorde wnto his kyndes, then in accidentes, whiche followeth the nature of them, Secondly for that he hath falne unto the same negligence That* [fol. 47ᵛ] *others did. in declaring how all*

---

[j] Friedrich Beurhaus, *Erotematum musicae libri duo* (1573), facs. ed. Walter Thoere (Beiträge zur rheinische Musikgeschichte, 47; Cologne: Arno Volk, 1961) (also see Hill, p. 13 n. 11).

[k] Othmar Luscinius (Nachtigall), *Musurgia seu praxis musicae* (Strasbourg: Johann Schott, 1536) (also see Hill, p. 13 n. 12).

concordes ar reduced. to the first 4. in so much, as he hath not shewed, how thes concordes which he hath not numbred, ar to be reduced, thirdly, for that he sheveth not a sufficient reasone for the denomination of the concordes perfect, or vnperfect: albeit I know Ottomarus *his reasone wil suffice many: as it would suffice many, that ye fire should be called hoat, because it heateth, which is fals and ewen as the fire is named hoat, of the heat which it hath In it selff, and heating of the heat oractione proceiding from it, so the concordes ar called perfect, of the perfection that they hawe in them selves. and perfecting, by that reasone which* Ottomarus *sheweth. Moreouer, by this reasone a third and tenth micht be called perfect, bicaus songes oft end with them, and this himselff denyeth. but the sound of them is called perfect, becauss it admitteth no variatione: so that this reason is conuerted with a perfect concord: for whatsoeuer admitteth no variation is a perfect concord, and whatsoewer is a perfect concord, admitteth no variatione,*

Obiection

The logician saith, that ewerie diuision ought to be but of twa members, if it may so Be as well: but ottomarus *mad this diuisione of two members, as well: therfor he did best mok it,*

[fol. 48ʳ]
Solution

It is to be vnderstoode, that perfect and vnperfyt, wherof we haue sufficiently spokin befoir, are but accidents always consequents to the nature of the concords, evin as deorsum *and* in sublime ferri, *are accidents to the nature of the* <illegible text crossed out> <doersum> elements: *And as philosophers doo rather choose to say:* elementorum aliud aer, aliud aqua, aliud terra, *then* elementorum, aliud deorsum, aliud in sublime fertur: *so certenlye our devisione foure membred, is rather to be chosin, then the tuo membred of* Ottomarus, *wherfore he hath not so well dividit it:* etiam si hoc, tibi exemplum sufficere non videtur, quia elementus est substantia, & concordia accidens: videas, vt primae qualitates dividuntur in quatuor, cum in duas dividi, secundum eorum accidentia potuissent.

Objection

It seimeth against the nature of the number, that a third should be an vnperfect concord: for according to the old sentence of Pythagoras, *the number of 3. is of all numbers the most perfect.* vnde & ab Aristotle numerus diuinus dicitur, Platoni item (quod æiunt) philosophorum deo contingit numerus annorum vitæ absolutissimus, nempe 81. qui numerus provenit ex novenario, in se multiplicato: nouenarius autem ex tribus constat ternariis, quae res platoni apud multos diuinitatis opinionem peperit. Item virgilius: numero deus impare gaudet.

[fol. 48ᵛ]
Solutione

It is not vnfyt, that one thing in diuerse respecte should be perfect, and vnperfect, so as that number is called perfect which is whol in much[1] sort that it admitteth no equall diuisione (ratione defereti)[m] *so in musick, that consort is called perfect, which admitteth no variatione* (ratione distantiæ) *that is in respect of the distance betwixt the parte, as for example: becaus that a fift is a perfect concord, and consisteth of 4. whol nots & a half, it must alwayes haue the sam distance for the quarter of a not, aboue or vnder, maketh it a discord, but the sixt because it is an vnperfect concord, it may consist ether of 5. whole notes or of 5. and a half: & so of the rest. therefor least we should siem to fall in to the sam negligence, it wer guid that we determine som what, And declare how this diuisionne mought be mad logicall, and artificall, in such ssort, that the kindis of all concordes might be numbred in it, and nothing superfluous: then after to determine, and exactly declare, how concordes ar reduced to one of thes which we will number. and first it wer not vnfit, that we should diuid the distinct sound betwixt pairts, and then orderly by subdiuisione to come to the diuision of concords. the distinct soundes betwixt pairts, which hath no affinitie one with another, ar 7. that is to say ane vnizon, a second, a third, a fourth, a fifth, a sixt, and a seuenth. wherof ther be foure with ther kinds, to wit ane wnizon, a third, a fyft, and a sixt: wheirof ye wnizon* [fol. 49r] *and fift with the concordes of their kindes be perfect, the other two with their kinds vnperfect.*

To number mor concordes than thes wer superfloues, for aboue thes ther is no reasone why the diuisione should be ended at one concord mor than at another, and of this commeth it that one musitian saith, that ther are 15. concordes, another saith ther be 20. in so much as betwixt them ther is no agrement.

But to know by this our diuisione all concords it is to be vnderstood that quhatsoeuer is mad vp by adding 7. or seuens to any of thes, is a concord of that kind to which the 7 or sevines are added: as for example, 7 added to ane wnizon maketh eighth: twys, 7. added to the same maketh fyftein; thryce, sevin maketh two and twentie: which be all concordes of one kind with the vnizone, and so by ading 7. or sewens to each one of the other, the concords of their kindes are knowne.

---

[1] Possibly *such*.
[m] Possibly *deferenti*.

A breife conclusion to know the distance according to the account of notes

ALSO *it wer not wnfit, that now in ye end for the more certentie, we should declare the true distance, according to the certaine account of notes themselues, of whiche everie concord doth consist whiche is thus, The wnizon alwayes is in one place: The third doth consist of 2 notes and a halff, and sometymes of thrie, the fyft alwayes of four notes and a halff, the sixt sometymes of 5 notes, and sometymes of fyue notes and ane half, as the* [fol. 49ᵛ] *concordes of their kindes that ar counted acording to the Gamut, ar mad vp by additione of* <illegible text crossed out> *7: so the concords of the first 4. kindes acording to the account of wholl notes, ar maid vp by additione of 6. to the aforesaid: as the adding 6 to ane vnizone maketh 7. wherof the 8. according to that accom*pt *of Gamut doth consist. and so of the rest, Mark well this last conclusione, and pass no ouer it with a superficiall wiew: for trevlie by it, ye richt distance may soon be knaven, mervell not of me neverthe les, for keiping this long discours befor, in teling the richt distanc according to ye places in* gamut. *for I haw done yat cheifflie for 2 causes: vherof ye one is becaus yat according to yat account notes have thair denominationne: ye other is, that ye learner sould haue ye knavledg yerof: creidit me, you may cum to many yat haue studit yis science a long tym, yea, yat be verrie weill skillid in setting, quho for lak of ye knavledge of this conclusionne, wyll tak a concord to be a discord; they ar so adicted to ye places, quhich is a great feblying of ye first foundationn, q*uen *they cannot knav a concord from a discord. If yov vold try this that I say, disire any such, to sing fa in* f fa vt: *& sing yow for yat a not in* C sol fa vt *scharp, and ask him, vhat concord is it, and belive me yow sall find mor yat will say it is a discord, then that will say it is a concord (as it is indeide) for as I said befor; It is a saxt becaus it is of ye sam distance yat tav vther places in ye* gam vt *ar of, as* a re, *and* f fa vt, *and becas yat* [fol. 50ʳ] *evrie saxt doth consist of fiwe vholl notes, as thes do, or of fiw notes & a halff: and evrie thing yat consist of fiw notes, or fiwe notes and a halff, is a saxt (as apereth by the last conclusionne) bot ye names to quhich the ar greatlie adicted, deseveth tham, and this mark veill.*

In this science as in vtheres, it var guid yat from the begining to ye end we sould proceid gradatime, observing yat order quhich to ye learner will most induce: ye nmber of concordes & discordes being knaven by ye aforced roules, it now foloath yat ve sould tell of ye richt placing and order of tham; for quch in the beginning it var best yat ye learner did get sume plain songes, quhich he sould hav as a founddationne: then to mak vpon it concordis (as I will heireftor declare.)

The first kynde of vay yat is vsed to be maid, is to mak on concord for evrie not of ye plain song, quhich is called counter poynt, in quhich certain roules *ar to be observed, vherof, ye first and cheifest is, yat twa perfect conncordes of on kynd sould not be maid asending or discending to gieder: as two vnisones, two fyftis, vi*th *ye concordes of ther kyndis: for this genarallie in all places must be observid, though they be perfyt concordis, neveryeles two of yam, in the ordor aforced, will not doo weill: two notis in on place in counter poynt, vhen the plain song doth also stand, is not to be vsed: for albeit, yat it be not so evell, bot it may be tollearated, neveryeles, becaus it doth declair the sleuth, rather than ye diligence of ye maker, it is to be eschued vnles it be in 2 pairtis in on, or in mantaining a poynt, heir is it to be noted, ya*t *mantanig a point is a thing in musik very* [fol. 50ᵛ] *delectable; & sueit to ye eare, vhich is nothing else but to keepe ye same quantitie, ascentione & descentione of notes in on poynt yat ar in an other, eather in one place, vhen ye plainsong is not like, or in diuers, as for exampelle:*

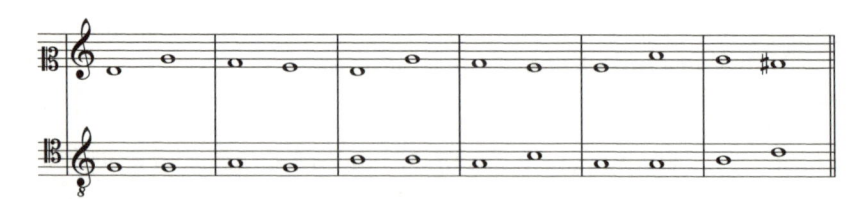

It being determined of two partes vhen they both stoode, It nov followeth that ve tell of the vther maner of going of tham, vherfor let this dewision suffice: the parts not standing both, must either goe against one an other, the on ascending, the other descending or on of tham must stande, the other ascending or descending, or both must ascend or descend togither: for ye first (that is to say) q*uen the go on against an other, it is naught to mak a fift, or any of yat kinde generallye, or an vnizon, or any of that kind vnles they com farther one against an other, or sometymes vhen ye next note to that vnizon or any of his kind of ye plaine song, doe stand in the same place. in the next vay, yat is to say vhen one standeth, the other ascending or descending, the fift is good, for ye latter of ye two standing notes, and not else vhich may be eather vhen these 2 notes that stande so, ar in ye plainesonge, or in the other partes as for examplle*

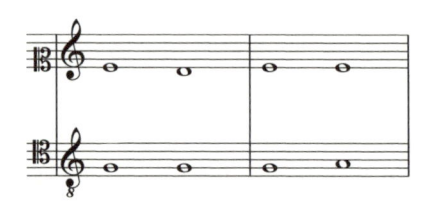

[fol. 51ʳ]
<illegible text crossed out> *The thrid way is quen both partes ascend or descend togither: vhich is 2 manner of wayes, eyther to ascend or descend farther than to ye next place vhich is called iumpyng: & not to be vsed in counterpoint or orderly & so 2 thrids 2. sixts, or 2 concordes of thair kindis, or 3 at ye most are to be vsed, last of all, observe that yow end not vith a sixt, or a concord of this kynd.*

Heir I haue briefflie comprehended the prohibitions, vhich I thought most likly the learner vod be apt to violate or breake (quich being observed) though they be bot fewe, I doubt not bot by gods grace they will cause the schoving of such faultes as by long protes[n] *common teacheris vse to prohibit: for indeid if a man did com through thair handes, and efter com to ye studie of other liberall sciences so far that he might sie in* quhat *darknes he hath bin occupied, I do not think (be he never so hard harted) bot it vald greiue him, I am suer moreover, that (as ye philosopher saith)* Omnes apetunt scire, *and he truely is wnworthy of his desyre, if he may)*[o] *thus much for counterpoint.*

The *next way that commonly is taught is called 2. minimes, which in this doth differ from the former way, that in making this, The maker is not limited to make on concord only for everie note of the plane song, as in counterpoint but at libertye to divide it wnto as many pairtes as the quantitie of the plaine song note serveth for; In this kynd of way, it is good always to begine with some rest: for the ascention and descention of 2 perfect concordes of one kynd, ther neideth no new prohibition: in so muche as I said befoir that in all kynd of descant it is naught: In counterpoint becaus it is note for note of the plainesong ether former divisione for* [fol. 51ᵛ] *The concourse of the pairtis sufficeth: but becaus that in 2. minims ther is alteratione of descant for ane not of plainsong it is necessary that ane other diuisione should be mad which is thus: if ther be any diuision, whatsoeuer not of descant is mad for any of plainesonge note must either Be for the first pairt of the note, Or els for that whiche is betuix ye first and last, Or otherwayes for the last pairt,*

For thes concordes that ar to be mad for the first part of any not, the comming from an other not to it, is Greatly to be regarded. It is guid alwais to begine with some rest. then for the comming from any other not to the first part of ewery not. yow must obserue the prohibitions of counterpoint, sawing that when the partes com one against another orderly, yow may mak ane eight or a concord of his kind, though they come not further one against ane other, or the next stand in the same place. Her is to be noted neuertheless, that to jumpe downe to an eight, and go vp from it Immedatly againe, is not to be vsed: except also somtymes for the first of a not a discord is vsed: but commonly either binding, or with a prick as for example:

---

[n] Possibly *protest*.

[o] No opening parentheses in MS 28. It is possible that this passage should read '*wnworthy of his desyre (if he may) thus much for counterpoint*'.

[fol. 52ʳ]

But from the first plainsong not to the end yow ar not tied to the rules of cunterpoint: but may mak what concord yow list: so that the descant be formal, which is alwayes to be obserued: neuertheles I hawe diuided the note Into 3 partes bacaus that for the other 2 parts, discords more commonlye ar vsed bot more seldome for the last pairt of the note, wnles it be in quaveris whiche in some respect may be discords for any pairt of the note, Thes manye wayes discords ar nought: First *when it is moir then a minim,* Secondlye *when they ar 2 of them together,* Thirdly *To iumpe from a concord to a discord, or from a discord to a concord wnles it be in the midle pairt of the note, and then iumping to the next saue one Wnder it, & best with Binding descant, or With a prick befoir it: as for exa[m]ple,*

Fourthllye *when the concords yat are in eache syde of it be aboue it,* Fyftlye *to mak it for the last pairt of any note, wnles the plaine songe stand or goe against it, the discorde being bot a croatchet, as for example.*

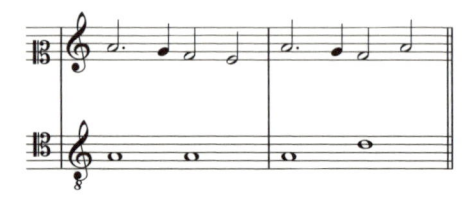

Their be discords that be not to be used perhaps, that by thes briefe rules ar not prohibited, Also there be things here prohibited, whiche manye doe vse to mak, Bot for that Trahit sua quemque voluptas. *For we more regarding that whiche doth to the learner bring most facilitie, and whiche are to be observed guid, haue laid doune suche breiff rules as we thought most necessary to that effeact, leaving the rest to the Imitatione of guid authors, as* M. talis, M. Byrd M. tailor *and others.*

Notes

1 Hawkins, *A General History of the Science and Practice of Music*, 497–99.
2 Cecil Hill, introduction to Bathe, *A Briefe Introductione to the True Art of Musicke* (Colorado Springs: Colorado College Press, 1979) (hereafter cited as Hill), p. i.
3 Robert Steele, *The Earliest English Music Printing* (London: Chadwick Press, 1903; repr. Meisenheim: Hain, 1965), 99.
4 There are two sources that preserve small portions of Bathe's text: Hawkins cited the title page (including publisher's imprint) and a portion of the preface (*A General History of the Science and Practice of Music*, 497); the title page alone is listed in Andrew Maunsell, *The Seconde Parte of the Catalogue of English Printed Bookes* (London: James Roberts, 1595), 16. Maunsell's citation is mentioned in Steele, *The Earliest English Music Printing*, 101.
5 William Walker, *Extracts from the Commonplace Book of Andrew Melville, Doctor and Master in the Song School of Aberdeen 1621–1640* (Aberdeen: John Rae Smith, 1899).
6 Ibid., p. xv.
7 Helena M. Shire, 'Andro Melvill's Music Library: Aberdeen, 1637 (Court Song in Scotland after 1603: Aberdeenshire – III)', in *Edinburgh Bibliographical Society Transactions*, 4, pt. 1 (1955–56) (Edinburgh: R. & R. Clark, 1960), 7.
8 Ibid., 10–11.
9 On the commonplace book more generally as both pedagogical aid and intellectual record, see Judd, *Reading Renaissance Music Theory*, 128–30.
10 The complete contents of the commonplace book are listed in Walker, *Extracts from the Commonplace Book of Andrew Melville*, pp. ii–xv. Walker omits two items from his list, both of which are musical transcriptions: the 'Toone of the Bells' (fol. 81^r) and the canticle *Nunc dimittis servum Tuum domine* (fol. 81^v).
11 These passages from Bathe's text are cited in Hawkins, *A General History of the Science and Practice of Music*, 497. They are included, with a note about their source, in the extant text of Bathe's treatise provided below.
12 Judd, *Reading Renaissance Music Theory*, 128–30.
13 Shire, 'Andro Melvill's Music Library', 5–7.
14 On the history of the school and Melville's tenure there, see Walker, *Extracts from the Commonplace Book of Andrew Melville*, pp. xvi–xlvi.
15 A similar point has previously been made in Hill, p. iii. Also revealing in this regard is the fact Melville seems to have taken several days to copy Bathe's treatise, as indicated by periodic variations in the handwriting on the relevant pages of the commonplace book.
16 *Cantus, Songs and Fancies. To Thre, Foure, or Five Partes, both apt for Voices and Viols* (Aberdeen: John Forbes, 1662) [Wing D379].
17 Ibid., sigs. ¶1^v–¶¶¶¶2^v. On Davidson's tenure at the Song School, see Walker, *Extracts from the Commonplace Book of Andrew Melville*, pp. xxxvii–xxxix.
18 Explaining the gamut to his readers, Davidson (or Forbes) writes: 'For the understanding of this foregoing Scale, you must begine at the lowest word, *Gam-ut*, and so go upwards to the end, still ascending. Then you must get it perfectly without Booke, to say it forewards and backwards. Secondly you must learn to know the Parts of it, and wherein every key standeth, that is, whether in Rule, or in Space. Thirdly, how many Cliefs and how many Notes every key conteineth, and Lastly, The Properties of the Gamme' (*Cantus, Songs and Fancies*, sig. ¶2^v). The source for this passage is Morley, *A Plaine and Easie Introduction to Practicall Musicke*, 3 (Harman, 10–12): 'For the vnderstanding of this Table, *You must begin at the lowest word* Gam-vt, *and*

so go vpwards to the end still ascending.... Then must you get it perfectly without booke, to saie it forwards and backwards. Secondly, *You must learne to knowe, wherein euery Key standeth*, that is, whether in rule or in space. And thirdly, *How manie cliefes and how manie notes euery Key containeth.*' As Owens has found, the italicized portions of Morley's discussion appear to be taken from Bathe's *A Briefe Introduction to the Skill of Song* (Owens, 'Concepts of Pitch', 200–201). It is clear in this case that Davidson's source was Morley, not Bathe. Davidson borrows similarly from Morley's treatise throughout sigs. ¶2ᵛ–¶¶1ᵛ. In her study of Melville's commonplace book, Shire notes that Morley's treatise is 'referred to' in Forbes's collection, but she does not elaborate on this point (Shire, 'Andro Melvill's Music Library', 8). Morley's name, however, does not appear to be mentioned in the collection.

[19] Hawkins's remarks on *A Briefe Introduction to the Skill of Song* are considered above, pp. 15–21.

[20] Hawkins, *A General History of the Science and Practice of Music*, 497–98.

[21] Owens, 'Concepts of Pitch', 233. This view is perpetuated in the new *English Short Title Catalogue* CD-ROM (The British Library and Eureka Research Libraries Group, 2000), where *A briefe introduction to the skill of song* is described as 'An edition of: A brief introduction to the true art of music'.

[22] Owens, 'Concepts of Pitch', 233.

[23] This aspect of Bathe's solmization method is discussed at length above, pp. 22–27.

[24] Maunsell, *The Seconde Parte of the Catalogue of English Printed Bookes*, 16; cited in Steele, *The Earliest English Music Printing*, 101.

[25] Hawkins, *A General History of the Science and Practice of Music*, 497.

[26] Jean F. Preston and Laetitia Yeandle, *English Handwriting 1400–1650: An Introductory Manual* (Asheville, NC: Pegasus Press, 1999).

Bibliography

Allaire, Gaston G., *The Theory of Hexachords, Solmization and the Modal System* (Musicological Studies and Documents, 24; n.p.: American Institute of Musicology, 1972).

Annibaldi, Claudio, 'Froberger in Rome: From Frescobaldi's Craftsmanship to Kircher's Compositional Secrets', *Current Musicology*, 58 (1995), 5–27.

—— 'La macchina dei cinque stili: nuovi documenti sul secondo soggiorno romano di Johann Jakob Froberger', in *La musica a Roma attraverso le fonti d'archivio. Atti del Convegno internazionale Roma 4–7 giugno 1992*, ed. Bianca Maria Antolini, Arnaldo Morelli and Vera Vita Spagnuolo (Strumenti della ricerca musicale collana della Società Italiana di Musicologia, 2; Lucca: Libreria musicale italiana, 1994), 399–408.

Apfel, Ernst, *Geschichte der Kompositionslehre: Von den Anfängen bis gegen 1700*, 3 vols (Taschenbücher zur Musikwissenschaft, 75–77; Wilhelmshaven: Heinrichshofen's Verlag, 1981).

Arber, Edward, *A Transcript of the Registers of the Company of Stationers of London, 1554–1640 A.D.*, 5 vols (London: n.p., 1875–94).

Bathe, William, *A Briefe Introduction to the Skill of Song* (London: Thomas Este, n.d.) [*STC* 1589]; facs., ed. Bernarr Rainbow (Kilkenny: Boethius Press, 1982; repr. Rochester, NY: University of Rochester Press, 1997).

—— *A Briefe Introductione to the True Art of Musicke* (London: Abell Jeffes, 1584 [lost]); ed. Cecil Hill (Colorado Springs: Colorado College Press, 1979).

Bent, Margaret, 'Diatonic Ficta', *Early Music History*, 4 (1984), 1–48.

—— 'Musica Recta and Musica Ficta', *Musica Disciplina*, 26 (1972), 73–100.

Berger, Christian, and Dean, Jeffrey J., 'Hexachord', in *MGG*, Sachteil, iv. 279–92.

Berger, Karol. *Musica ficta: Theories of Accidental Inflections in Vocal Polyphony from Marchetto da Padova to Gioseffo Zarlino* (Cambridge: Cambridge University Press, 1987).

Bevin, Elway, *A Briefe and Short Instruction of the Art of Musicke* (London: R. Young, 1635) [*STC* 1986].

Binns, J.W., 'John Case and "The Praise of Musicke"', *Music & Letters*, 55 (1974), 444–53.

Brady, Ciaran, *The Chief Governors: The Rise and Fall of Reform Government in Tudor Ireland, 1536–1588* (Cambridge Studies in Early Modern British History; Cambridge: Cambridge University Press, 1994).

Bryskett, Lodowick, *A Discovrse of Civill Life: Containing the Ethike Part of Morall Philosophie* (London: Edward Blount, 1606; facs., Amsterdam and New York: Da Capo Press, 1971).

Caldwell, John, *The Oxford History of English Music*, 2 vols (Oxford: Clarendon Press, 1991–99).

Campion, Thomas, *A New Way of Making Fowre Parts in Counter-Point* (London: Thomas Snodham, n.d.) [*STC* 4542]; ed. Walter R. Davis in *The Works of Thomas Campion: Complete Songs, Masques, and Treatises with a Selection of the Latin Verse* (Garden City, NY: Doubleday, 1967); ed. Christopher R. Wilson (Music Theory in Britain, 1500–1700: Critical Editions; Aldershot and Burlington, VT: Ashgate, 2003).

Cantus, Songs and Fancies. To Thre, Four, or Five Partes (Aberdeen: John Forbes, 1662) [Wing D379].

Castiglione, Baldassare, *The Courtyer of Count Baldessar Castilio. Done into Englyshe by [Sir] T[homas] Hoby* (London: William Seres, 1561; mod. edn, London: J.M. Dent and Sons, 1974).

Castronovo, David, *The English Gentleman: Images and Ideals in Literature and Society* (New York: Ungar, 1987).

Cochlaeus, Johannes, *Tetrachordum musices* (Nuremberg: Hans Stuchs, 1512); trans. and ed. Clement A. Miller (n.p.: American Institute of Musicology, 1970).

Cooper, Barry, 'Englische Musiktheorie im 17. und 18. Jahrhundert', in *Entstehung nationaler Traditionen: Frankreich-England* (Geschichte der Musiktheorie, 9; Darmstadt: Wissenschaftliche Buchgesellschaft, 1986), 141–314.

Corcoran, Timothy, *Studies in the History of Classical Teaching: Irish and Continental, 1500–1700* (New York: Benziger Brothers, 1911).

Cosyn, John, *Musike of Six, and Fiue Partes* (London: John Wolfe, 1585) [*STC* 5828].

Daman, William, *The Former Booke of the Musicke of M. William Damon* (London: Thomas East, 1591) [*STC* 6220]. *The second Booke* . . . (London: Thomas East, 1591) [*STC* 6221].

Edwards, Paul (ed.), *The Encyclopedia of Philosophy*, 9 vols (New York and London: Collier and Macmillan, 1967).

Ellis, Steven G., *Ireland in the Age of the Tudors, 1447–1603: English Expansion and the End of Gaelic Rule* (Longman History of Ireland; London and New York: Longman, 1998).

Elyot, Sir Thomas, *The Boke Named the Gouernour* (London: T. Bertholeti, 1531); ed. S.E. Lehmberg (New York: Dutton, 1962).

Farmer, John, *Diuers & sundry waies of two parts in one, to the number of fortie, vppon one playnsong* (London: Thomas East, 1591) [*STC* 10698].

Flynn, Jane, 'The Education of Choristers in England during the Sixteenth Century', in John Morehen (ed.), *English Choral Practice, 1400–1650*

(Cambridge Studies in Performance Practice; Cambridge: Cambridge University Press, 1995), 180–99.

—— 'A Reconsideration of the Mulliner Book (British Library Add. MS 30513): Music Education in Sixteenth-Century England' (Ph.D. diss., Duke University, 1993).

Fraunce, Abraham, *The Arcadian Rhetorike: Or the Praecepts of Rhetorike Made Plaine by Examples* (London: Thomas Orwin, 1588) [*STC* 11338].

Gosman, Alan, 'Stacked Canon and Renaissance Compositional Procedure', *Journal of Music Theory*, 41 (1997), 289–317.

Hankey, Susan, 'The Compleat Gentleman's Music', *Music & Letters*, 62 (1981), 146–54.

Hawkins, Sir John, *A General History of the Science and Practice of Music* (London, 1776; repr. London: J. Alfred Novello, 1853).

Henderson, Robert V., 'Solmization Syllables in Musical Theory, 1100–1600' (Ph.D. diss., Columbia University, 1969).

Herissone, Rebecca, *Music Theory in Seventeenth-Century England* (Oxford Monographs on Music; Oxford: Oxford University Press, 2000).

Heyden, Sebald, *De arte canendi* (Nuremberg: Petreius, 1540); trans. and ed. Clement A. Miller (n.p.: American Institute of Musicology, 1972).

Hunnis, William, *Seuen Sobs of a Sorrowfull Soule for Sinne* (London: Henry Denham, 1583) [*STC* 13975].

The Institucion of a Gentleman (London: Thomas Marshe, 1555; facs. Amsterdam and Norwood, NJ: Walter J. Johnson, 1974).

Johnson, Gerald, 'William Barley, "Publisher & Seller of Bookes"', *The Library*, ser. 6, vol. 11, no. 1 (1989), 10–46.

Johnson, Timothy A., 'Solmization in the English Treatises around the Turn of the Seventeenth Century: A Break from Modal Theory', *Theoria*, 5 (1990–91), 42–60.

Judd, Cristle Collins, *Reading Renaissance Music Theory: Hearing with the Eyes* (Cambridge Studies in Music Theory and Analysis, 14; Cambridge: Cambridge University Press, 2000).

Kircher, Athanasius, *Musurgia vniversalis sive ars magna consoni et dissoni in X. libros digesta*, i (Rome: Francisci Corbelletti, 1650); ii (Rome: Ludovici Grignani, 1650; facs. (in one volume) ed. Ulf Scharlau: Hildesheim and New York: Georg Olms, 1970).

Krummel, Donald W., *English Music Printing, 1553–1700* (London: The Bibliographical Society, 1975).

Lampadius, Auctor, *Compendium musices, tam figurati quam plani cantus ad formam Dialogi* (Bern: Mathias Apiarius, 1541).

Lossius, Lucas. *Erotemata musicae practicae* (Nuremberg: Johann Berg and Ulrich Neuber, 1563; facs., Bologna: Arnaldo Forni, n.d.).

Lusitano, Vicente, *Introduttione facilissima, et novissima, di canto fermo, figurato, contraponto semplice, et in concerto* (Venice: Francesco Rampazetto, 1553; facs. ed. Giuliana Gialdroni, Rome: Libreria musicale italiana, 1989).

Mason, Philip, *The English Gentleman: The Rise and Fall of an Ideal* (New York: William Morrow and Company, 1982).

Maunsell, Andrew, *The Second Parte of the Catalogue of English Printed Bookes* (London: James Roberts, 1595) [*STC* 17669].

McDonald, Walter, 'Irish Ecclesiastical Colleges since the Reformation. Salamanca – III', *Irish Ecclesiastical Record*, ser. 2, vol. 10 (1873–74), 519–32.

Miller, Hugh Milton, 'Forty Wayes of 2 Pts. in One of Tho[mas] Woodson', *Journal of the American Musicological Society*, 8 (1955), 14–21.

Miller, Miriam, and Smith, Jeremy L., 'Thomas East', in *New Grove II*, vii. 836–37.

Morley, Thomas, *A Plaine and Easie Introduction to Practicall Musicke* (London: Peter Short, 1597; facs., Amsterdam and New York: Da Capo Press, 1969); ed. Alec Harman (New York: W.W. Norton & Company, 1952).

Moseley, C.W.R.D., 'The Lost Play of Mandeville', *The Library*, ser. 5, vol. 25 (1970), 46–49.

Ó Mathúna, Seán P., *William Bathe, S. J., 1564–1614: A Pioneer in Linguistics* (Amsterdam Studies in the Theory and History of Linguistic Science, 37; Amsterdam and Philadelphia: John Benjamins Publishing Company, 1986).

O'Malley, John W., *The First Jesuits* (Cambridge, Mass.: Harvard University Press, 1993).

Owens, Jessie Ann, 'Concepts of Pitch in English Music Theory, c. 1560–1640', in Cristle Collins Judd (ed.), *Tonal Structures in Early Music* (New York: Garland, 1998), 183–246.

The Pathvvay to Musicke (London: William Barley, 1596) [*STC* 19464].

Peacham, Henry, *The Compleat Gentleman* (London: Francis Constable, 1622; facs., Amsterdam and New York: Da Capo Press, 1968).

The Praise of Musicke (Oxford: Joseph Barnes, 1586; facs., Hildesheim and New York: Georg Olms, 1980).

Preston, Jean F., and Yeandle, Laetitia, *English Handwriting 1400–1650: An Introductory Manual* (Asheville, NC: Pegasus Press, 1999).

Preußner, Eberhard, 'Solmisationsmethoden im Schulunterricht des 16. und 17. Jahrhunderts', in Hans Hoffmann and Franz Rühlemann (eds.), *Festschrift Fritz Stein zum 60. Geburtstag* (Braunschweig: H. Litolff, 1939), 112–28.

Price, David C., *Patrons and Musicians of the English Renaissance* (Cambridge Studies in Music; Cambridge: Cambridge University Press, 1981).

Rainbow, Bernarr, *English Psalmody Prefaces: Popular Methods of Teaching, 1562–1835* (Kilkenny: Boethius Press, 1982).

Rainolde, Richard, *A Booke Called the Foundacion of Rhetorike* (London: John Kingston, 1563) [*STC* 20604].

Robinson, Thomas, *The Schoole of Musicke: Wherein is Taught, the Perfect Method, of True Fingering of the Lute, Pandora, Orpharion, and Viol de Gamba* (London: Thomas East, 1603; facs., Amsterdam and New York: Da Capo Press, 1973).

Sherrye, Richarde, *A Treatise of the Figures of Grammer and Rhetorike* (London: Ricardi Totteli, 1555) [*STC* 22429].

Shire, Helena M., 'Andro Melvill's Music Library: Aberdeen, 1637 (Court Song in Scotland after 1603: Aberdeenshire – III)', in *Edinburgh Bibliographical Society Transactions*, 4, pt. 1 (Session 1955–56) (Edinburgh: R. & R. Clark, 1960), 1–12.

Simpson, Christopher, *A Compendium of Practical Musick in Five Parts*, 2nd edn (London: William Godbid, 1667); ed. Phillip J. Lord (Oxford: Basil Blackwell, 1970).

Smith, Jeremy L., 'From "Rights to Copy" to the "Bibliographic Ego": A New Look at the Last Early Edition of Byrd's "Psalmes, Sonets & Songs"', *Music & Letters*, 80 (1999), 511–30.

—— 'The Hidden Editions of Thomas East', *Notes: The Quarterly Journal of the Music Library Association,* 53, no. 4 (1997), 1059–91.

—— *Thomas East and Music Publishing in Renaissance England* (Oxford and New York: Oxford University Press, 2003).

Steele, Robert, *The Earliest English Music Printing* (London: Chadwick Press, 1903; repr. Meisenheim: Hain, 1965).

Temperley, Nicholas, *The Hymn Tune Index: A Census of English-Language Hymn Tunes in Printed Sources from 1535 to 1820*, 4 vols (Oxford: Clarendon Press, 1998).

—— *Music of the English Parish Church*, 2 vols (Cambridge Studies in Music; Cambridge: Cambridge University Press, 1979).

Walker, William, *Extracts from the Commonplace Book of Andrew Melville, Doctor and Master in the Song School of Aberdeen 1621–1640* (Aberdeen: John Rae Smith, 1899).

The Whole Booke of Psalmes, Collected into Englysh Metre by T. Starnhold I. Hopkins & Others (London: John Day, 1562) [*STC* 2430]; (London: John Day, 1569) [*STC* 2439.5].

The Whole Booke of Psalmes: With Their Wonted Tunes (London: Thomas East, 1592) [*STC* 2483].

The Whole Psalmes in Foure Partes (London: John Day, 1563) [*STC* 2431].

Whythorne, Thomas, *The Autobiography of Thomas Whythorne* [manuscript]; ed. James M. Osborn (London: Oxford University Press, 1962).

—— *Duos, or Songs for Tvvo Voices* (London: Thomas East, 1590) [*STC* 25583].

Wienpahl, Robert W., *Music at the Inns of Court during the Reigns of Elizabeth, James, and Charles* (Ann Arbor: University Microfilms International, 1979).

Wilson, Thomas, *The Arte of Rhetorike* (London: John Kingston, 1563) [*STC* 25802].

Wood, Anthony, *Athenae Oxonienses. An Exact History of all the Writers and Bishops Who Have Had Their Education in the Most Ancient and Famous University of Oxford*, 4 vols (London: Thomas Bennet, 1691) [Wing W3382].

Index

Aberdeen
   Song School 101–2, 104–5
   University of 101–2
accidentals, *see* solmization
Allison, Richard 10
Anderson, John 101
Andrews, H.K. 48
Aristotle
   Post-Predicaments (from *Categories*) 22

Barley, William 3, 15
Beurhaus, Friedrich
   Erotematum musicae libri duo 120
Bevin, Elway
   A Briefe and Short Instruction in the Art of Musicke 52
Blancks, Edward 10–12, 71, 96
Bryskett, Lodowick 19, 20
Bull, John 102
Butler, Charles 102
Byrd, William 10, 12–13

Campion, Thomas
   A New Way of Making Fowre Parts in Counter-Point 24, 32, 102
canon 3, 32–42, 42–3, 52–3, 96–7, 78–81, 85–90; see also *Gladius Musicus*
Case, John 19
Castiglione, Baldassare
   The Courtyer 8, 46
Cochlaeus, Johannes
   Tetrachordum musices 51
Company of Stationers, London 4, 13–15
Cooper, Barry 44–5, 51
Corcoran, Timothy 6
Cosyn, John 10
counterpoint 42, 123–6

Daman, William 10
Davidson, Thomas 105, 127–8
Day, John 10, 17, 27–8
   The Whole Booke of Psalms 10, 17, 27–9, 51; see also solfège type
Day, Richard 10, 13

Dean, Jeffrey 51
Delamotte, P.
   A Brief Introduction to the True Art of Music 44–5
Denham, Henry 10
Dowland, John 10

East, Thomas 3, 4, 9–15, 47–8
   The Whole Booke of Psalmes: With Their Wonted Tunes 9–13
Elizabeth I 6
Elyot, Sir Thomas
   The Boke Named the Gouernour 8–9, 46

Farmer, John
   Diuers & Sundry Waies of Two Parts in One 32
Fitzwilliam, William 7
Flynn, Jane 48, 52
Forbes, John
   Cantus, Songs and Fancies 104–5, 127–8

Gladius Musicus (Bathe) 42, 80–81, 96–7
Gray's Inn, London 6

Hawkins, Sir John
   A General History of the Science and Practice of Music 6, 15–16, 18–19, 43, 101–2, 105, 111
Herissone, Rebecca 48, 93–4
hexachord, *see* solmization
Heyden, Sebald
   De arte canendi 25
Hill, Cecil 101–2, 111, 127
Hoby, Sir Thomas 8
Hunnis, William 10

Ianua linguarum (Bathe) 44
The Institucion of a Gentleman 8–9

Jeffes, Abell 3, 13–14
Jesuit Order, *see* Society of Jesus
Johnson, Timothy A. 24–5
Judd, Cristle Collins 48, 102

Index

key 32, 66
Kirbye, George 10–12, 83–4, 97
Kircher, Athanasius 33
Krummel, Donald W. 10, 13–14, 48

Lampadius, Auctor
   Compendium musices 49
Le Roy, Adrian
   A Briefe and Plaine Instruction to Set All Musicke of Eight Divers Tunes in Tableture for the Lute 44
Lossius, Lucas
   Erotemata musicae practicae 23–4, 49
Luscinius, Othmar
   Musurgia seu praxis musicae 120
Lusitano, Vicente
   Introduttione facilissima, et novissima 33

Manrique, Pedro (pseud. for Bathe) 44
Maunsell, Andrew
   Catalogue of English Printed Bookes 111
Melville, Andrew 101–5, 111
   Commonplace Book of 101–3, 127
Miller, Miriam 14
Morley, Thomas
   A Plaine and Easie Introduction to Practicall Musicke 3, 12, 17–18, 22, 24, 27, 31–5, 42–3, 45, 47, 50, 51, 102, 105, 127–8
Moseley, C. W. R. D. 47–8
'Musical Sword' (Bathe), *see* Gladius Musicus

'naming' (Bathe), *see* solmization

Ó Mathúna, Seán P. 6–7, 47
'order of ascension' (Bathe), *see* solmization
Owens, Jessie Ann 3, 9, 11, 15, 24–5, 27, 31–2, 46, 47, 105, 128
Oxford University 6, 9

The Pathvvay to Musicke 3, 12, 24, 45, 47
Peacham, Henry
   The Compleat Gentleman 8–9
Perrott, Lord Deputy John 6–7

Philip II 7
The Praise of Musicke 19–20

Ravenscroft, Thomas
   A Briefe Discourse of the True (But Neglected) Vse of Chact'ring the Degrees 102
rhetoric 16–21, 49
   objection and answer 18–21, 31–2, 49, 93–4
Robinson, Thomas
   The Schoole of Musicke 18
'The rule of Vt' (Bathe), *see* solmization

St John's College, Oxford 6
Sherlock, Paul 4
Sherrye, Richarde
   Treatise of the Figures of Grammer and Rhetorike 19–20
Shire, Helena 101–2
Short, Peter 3, 15
Simpson, Christopher
   Compendium of Practical Music 43
Smith, Jeremy L. 3, 4, 10, 12, 13–15, 48
Society of Jesus 4, 6, 45
solfège type 27, 51
solmization 3, 22–32, 60–66, 72, 93–6, 113–15, 116–18; *see also* key; solfège type
   accidentals, tuning of 29–32, 64–6, 68–70, 94–6
   hexachordal 16, 23–5, 27–9
   'naming' pitches (Bathe) 24, 28–32, 61–6, 72, 113–15
   'order of ascension' (Bathe) 24–5, 27–31, 61, 93
   'The rule of Vt' (Bathe) 23, 25–7, 29–31, 93
Steele, Robert 101
'Sternhold and Hopkins' metrical psalter, *see* John Day, *The Whole Booke of Psalmes*

Temperley, Nicholas 10
'tuning' (Bathe), *see* solmization
'two parts in one', *see* canon

Walker, William 101
Whythorne, Thomas 3, 9, 46, 47
   Duos, or Songs for Tvvo Voices 32

Wilson, Thomas
The Arte of Rhetorike 20

Wolfe, John 10, 14
Wood, Anthony 45–6